Multiplication and Division Drills

Grades 4-6

Written and Illustrated by S&S Learning Materials

ISBN 1-55035-755-7
Copyright 2004
Revised January 2006
All Rights Reserved * Printed in Canada

Published in the United States by:
On the Mark Press
3909 Witmer Road PMB 175
Niagara Falls, New York
14305
www.onthemarkpress.com

Published in Canada by:
S&S Learning Materials
15 Dairy Avenue
Napanee, Ontario
K7R 1M4
www.sslearning.com

© On The Mark Press • S&S Learning Materials

OTM-1132 • SSK1-32 Multiplication &
Division Drills

Two Methods for Mastering Multiple-Digit Multiplication

1. Traditional Method (with 2- and 3-Digit Factors)

Multiplication with multiple-digit numbers involves the three steps of multiplying, carrying and adding. In the traditional method of multiplication, these steps are combined which demands flexibility in higher-level thinking.

Example: 634 x 25 = ?

Begin by multiplying the ones value (5) of the 2-digit factor (25) with the ones value (4) of the 3-digit factor (634). Repeat this step by multiplying the 5 with the *tens* value (3), and then by the *hundreds* value (6) of the 3-digit factor. Whenever the product of each of these steps is more than a single digit, be sure to carry the tens value [see calculation a)]. Then repeat all of a), this time multiplying the tens value (2) of the 2-digit factor (25) by the ones, tens and hundreds values respectively of the 3-digit factor [calculation b)]. Complete the problem by adding the partial products from a) and b) [calculation c)].

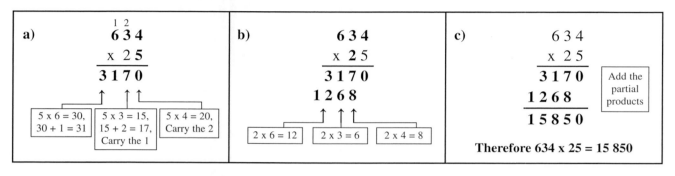

2. Lattice Method (with 2- and 3-Digit Factors)

This procedure allows students to solve a multiple-digit multiplication problem in smaller, more manageable steps than those required for the traditional method. The steps of multiplying, carrying and adding are done separately in this method, making the calculations easier to do. A grid or "lattice" is used as a framework, and each product that is calculated for the single-digit factors is record in a box within the lattice. In each box, the tens digit is recorded above the diagonal line and the ones digit is recorded below [see diagram a)].

Example: 634 x 25 = ?

Begin by drawing a grid of 3 columns by 2 rows, and write the numerals for the 3-digit factor across the top and the numerals for the 2-digit factor down the right side [diagram b).] Now multiply each single digit of one factor with each single digit of the other factor, beginning with 4 x 2. Partial products that are only one digit should be recorded with a zero in the tens place [calculations c) and d)]. Complete the problem by adding along the diagonals from right to left in order to find the final product. Any tens values that are "carried" are recorded outside the grid [calculation e)].

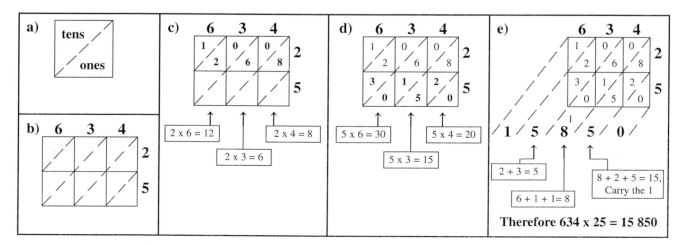

Multiplication Drill Work Sheets

Name: _____

Skill: Picture Multiplication

Start With	Multiply By	Equals

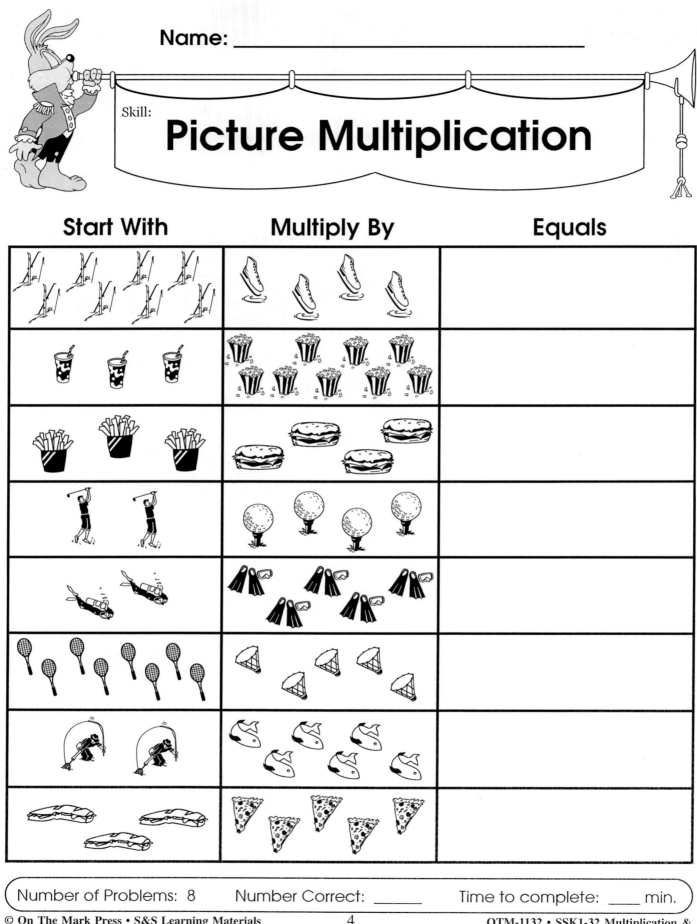

Number of Problems: 8   Number Correct: _____   Time to complete: ____ min.

© On The Mark Press • S&S Learning Materials   4   OTM-1132 • SSK1-32 Multiplication & Division Drills

Skill:

Multiplication x0

9 x 0	7 x 0	1 x 0	5 x 0	12 x 0
6 x 0	3 x 0	8 x 0	11 x 0	2 x 0
4 x 0	10 x 0	12 x 0	1 x 0	8 x 0
4 x 0	2 x 0	10 x 0	9 x 0	7 x 0
1 x 0	9 x 0	7 x 0	5 x 0	11 x 0
6 x 0	5 x 0	12 x 0	3 x 0	8 x 0

Number of Problems: 30   Number Correct: _____   Time to complete: ____ min.

Name: _____

Skill:

Multiplication x1

6	2	9	1	12
x 1	x 1	x 1	x 1	x 1

3	10	7	11	4
x 1	x 1	x 1	x 1	x 1

5	8	12	3	9
x 1	x 1	x 1	x 1	x 1

1	6	4	10	8
x 1	x 1	x 1	x 1	x 1

5	2	11	7	3
x 1	x 1	x 1	x 1	x 1

12	6	9	4	8
x 1	x 1	x 1	x 1	x 1

Number of Problems: 30   Number Correct: _____   Time to complete: ____ min.

Skill:

Multiplication x2

7 x 2	1 x 2	12 x 2	9 x 2	3 x 2
2 x 2	10 x 2	6 x 2	11 x 2	4 x 2
5 x 2	8 x 2	12 x 2	1 x 2	6 x 2
3 x 2	7 x 2	9 x 2	4 x 2	10 x 2
5 x 2	2 x 2	8 x 2	1 x 2	12 x 2
9 x 2	4 x 2	3 x 2	7 x 2	10 x 2

Number of Problems: 30   Number Correct: _____   Time to complete: ____ min.

Skill:

Multiplication x3

1 x 3	11 x 3	7 x 3	5 x 3	2 x 3
6 x 3	10 x 3	3 x 3	12 x 3	8 x 3
4 x 3	9 x 3	5 x 3	8 x 3	1 x 3
6 x 3	10 x 3	2 x 3	9 x 3	4 x 3
3 x 3	7 x 3	11 x 3	1 x 3	10 x 3
12 x3	3 x 3	6 x 3	9 x 3	2 x 3

Number of Problems: 30   Number Correct: _____   Time to complete: ____ min.

Name: _____

Skill:

Multiplication x4

9 x 4	12 x 4	1 x 4	6 x 4	8 x 4
2 x 4	10 x 4	5 x 4	11 x 4	3 x 4
4 x 4	7 x 4	12 x 4	2 x 4	5 x 4
8 x 4	6 x 4	11 x 4	9 x 4	4 x 4
3 x 4	7 x 4	10 x 4	1 x 4	2 x 4
8 x 4	3 x 4	12 x 4	4 x 4	9 x 4

Number of Problems: 30   Number Correct: _____   Time to complete: ____ min.

Name: _____

Multiplication x5

8 x 5	1 x 5	3 x 5	12 x 5	2 x 5
7 x 5	4 x 5	11 x 5	9 x 5	6 x 5
10 x 5	5 x 5	7 x 5	2 x 5	6 x 5
5 x 5	11 x 5	4 x 5	8 x 5	1 x 5
3 x 5	9 x 5	12 x 5	5 x 5	8 x 5
7 x 5	9 x 5	10 x 5	1 x 5	3 x 5

Number of Problems: 30   Number Correct: _____   Time to complete: ____ min.

Name: _____

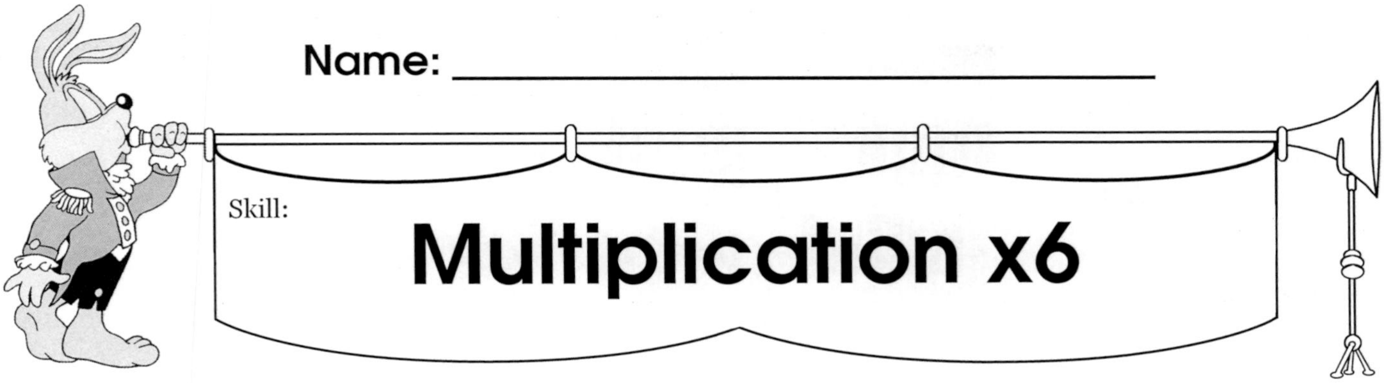

Skill:

Multiplication x6

6 x 6	1 x 6	8 x 6	5 x 6	12 x 6
9 x 6	10 x 6	3 x 6	7 x 6	2 x 6
11 x 6	4 x 6	8 x 6	12 x 6	1 x 6
7 x 6	10 x 6	5 x 6	12 x 6	9 x 6
11 x 6	1 x 6	6 x 6	4 x 6	8 x 6
9 x 6	12 x 6	7 x 6	2 x 6	5 x 6

Number of Problems: 30   Number Correct: _____   Time to complete: ____ min.

Name: _____

Skill:

Multiplication x7

5 x 7	12 x 7	1 x 7	3 x 7	10 x 7
9 x 7	2 x 7	6 x 7	8 x 7	4 x 7
7 x 7	11 x 7	2 x 7	5 x 7	8 x 7
6 x 7	1 x 7	3 x 7	12 x 7	4 x 7
9 x 7	11 x 7	7 x 7	10 x 7	9 x 7
7 x 7	5 x 7	12 x 7	1 x 7	3 x 7

Number of Problems: 30   Number Correct: _____   Time to complete: ____ min.

Name: _____

Skill:

Multiplication x8

5 x 8	9 x 8	12 x 8	3 x 8	7 x 8
1 x 8	6 x 8	2 x 8	11 x 8	8 x 8
10 x 8	4 x 8	1 x 8	3 x 8	5 x 8
8 x 8	11 x 8	6 x 8	2 x 8	9 x 8
7 x 8	4 x 8	10 x 8	12 x 8	7 x 8
5 x 8	1 x 8	8 x 8	12 x 8	9 x 8

Number of Problems: 30   Number Correct: _____   Time to complete: ____ min.

Name: _____

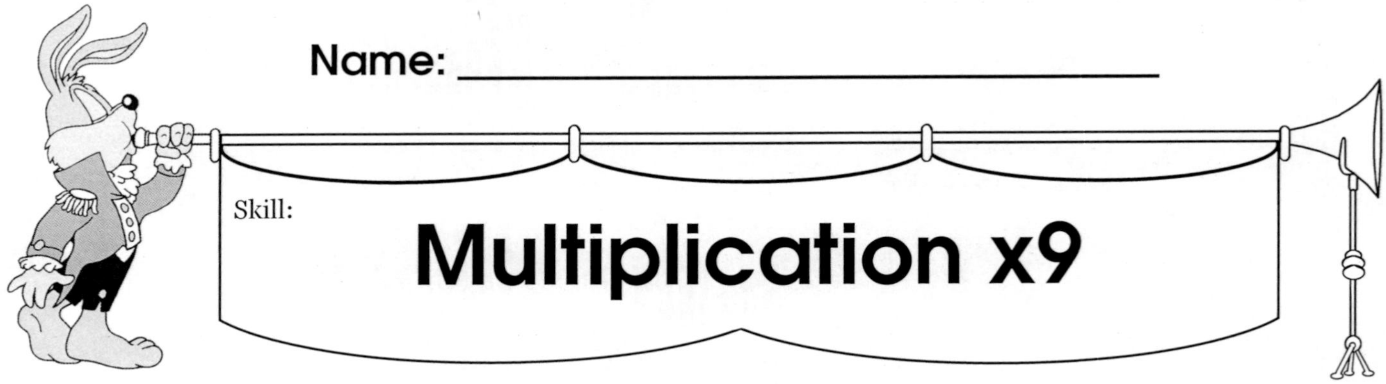

Skill:

Multiplication x9

9 x 9	12 x 9	5 x 9	1 x 9	6 x 9
7 x 9	10 x 9	2 x 9	4 x 9	8 x 9
3 x 9	11 x 9	7 x 9	5 x 9	12 x 9
4 x 9	8 x 9	11 x 9	2 x 9	6 x 9
1 x 9	10 x 9	3 x 9	9 x 9	8 x 9
5 x 9	12 x 9	9 x 9	7 x 9	3 x 9

Number of Problems: 30   Number Correct: _____   Time to complete: ____ min.

Name: _____

Skill:

Multiplication x10

8 x 10	5 x 10	3 x 10	9 x 10	1 x 10
2 x 10	10 x 10	7 x 10	4 x 10	12 x 10
11 x 10	6 x 10	3 x 10	7 x 10	4 x 10
9 x 10	10 x 10	2 x 10	6 x 10	5 x 10
8 x 10	1 x 10	11 x 10	7 x 10	10 x 10
2 x 10	5 x 10	7 x 10	12 x 10	4 x 10

Number of Problems: 30   Number Correct: _____   Time to complete: _____ min.

Name: _____

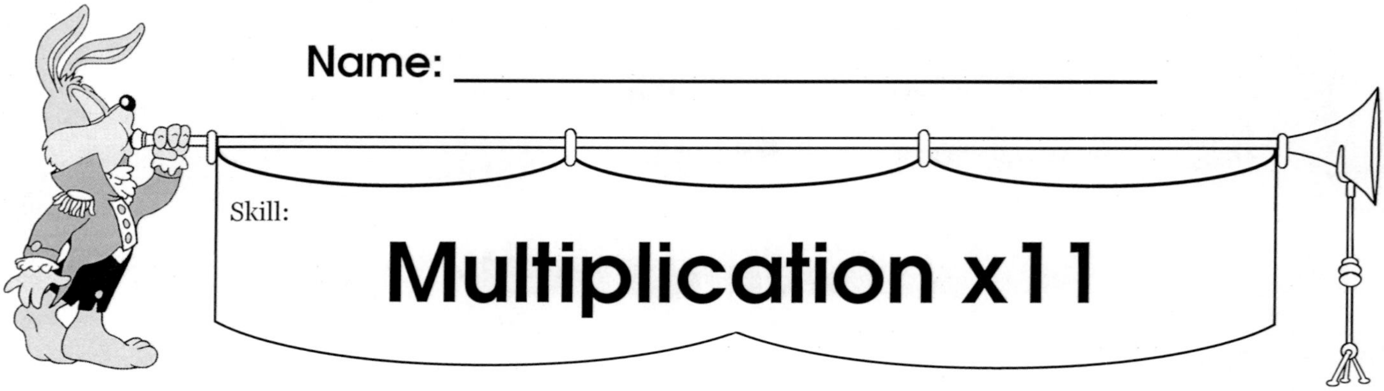

Multiplication x11

6 x 11	11 x 11	1 x 11	7 x 11	5 x 11
3 x 11	10 x 11	4 x 11	8 x 11	2 x 11
12 x 11	9 x 11	5 x 11	1 x 11	11 x 11
3 x 11	7 x 11	4 x 11	10 x 11	8 x 11
2 x 11	6 x 11	9 x 11	12 x 11	11 x 11
7 x 11	9 x 11	5 x 11	1 x 11	3 x 11

Number of Problems: 30   Number Correct: _____   Time to complete: ____ min.

Name: _____

Multiplication x12

12 x 12	7 x 12	4 x 12	1 x 12	9 x 12
5 x 12	2 x 12	11 x 12	3 x 12	8 x 12
10 x 12	6 x 12	7 x 12	5 x 12	10 x 12
9 x 12	12 x 12	3 x 12	1 x 12	6 x 12
8 x 12	11 x 12	4 x 12	10 x 12	2 x 12
5 x 12	7 x 12	12 x 12	3 x 12	9 x 12

Number of Problems: 30   Number Correct: _____   Time to complete: ____ min.

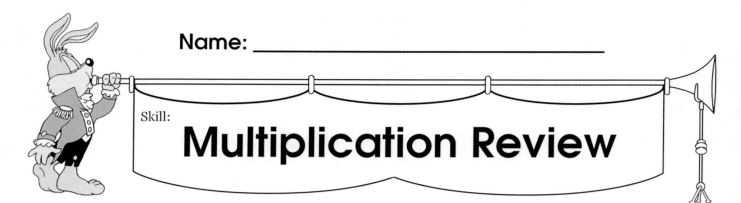

Name: _____

Multiplication Review

5 x 3 = _____	8 x 2 = _____	4 x 1 = _____
7 x 6 = _____	9 x 8 = _____	2 x 2 = _____
8 x 7 = _____	9 x 0 = _____	7 x 2 = _____
10 x 4 = _____	5 x 7 = _____	2 x 1 = _____
8 x 3 = _____	12 x 9 = _____	3 x 6 = _____
11 x 4 = _____	2 x 4 = _____	12 x 5 = _____
12 x 7 = _____	3 x 7 = _____	2 x 7 = _____
6 x 9 = _____	7 x 9 = _____	10 x 9 = _____
3 x 3 = _____	2 x 5 = _____	12 x 3 = _____
7 x 7 = _____	5 x 9 = _____	11 x 6 = _____
8 x 5 = _____	3 x 9 = _____	9 x 9 = _____
11 x 7 = _____	2 x 9 = _____	8 x 2 = _____

Number of Problems: 36   Number Correct: _____   Time to complete: ____ min.

Name: _____

Multiplication Table

	1	**2**	**3**	**4**	**5**	**6**	**7**	**8**	**9**	**10**	**11**	**12**
1	1	2	3	4	5	6	7	8	9	10	11	12
2	2	4	6	8	10	12	14	16	18	20	22	24
3	3	6	9	12	15	18	21	24	27	30	33	36
4	4	8	12	16	20	24	28	32	36	40	44	48
5	5	10	15	20	25	30	35	40	45	50	55	60
6	6	12	18	24	30	36	42	48	54	60	66	72
7	7	14	21	28	35	42	49	56	63	70	77	84
8	8	16	24	32	40	48	56	64	72	80	88	96
9	9	18	27	36	45	54	63	72	81	90	99	108
10	10	20	30	40	50	60	70	80	90	100	110	120
11	11	22	33	44	55	66	77	88	99	110	121	132
12	12	24	36	48	60	72	84	96	108	120	132	144

	1	**2**	**3**	**4**	**5**	**6**	**7**	**8**	**9**	**10**	**11**	**12**
1												
2												
3												
4												
5												
6												
7												
8												
9												
10												
11												
12												

OTM-1132 • SSK1-32 Multiplication & Division Drills

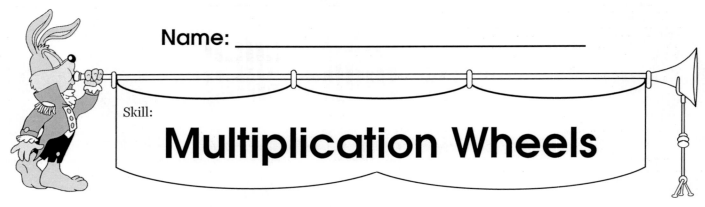

Skill:

Multiplication Wheels

Multiply the number in the middle with each number in turn. Then write your answer in the blank.

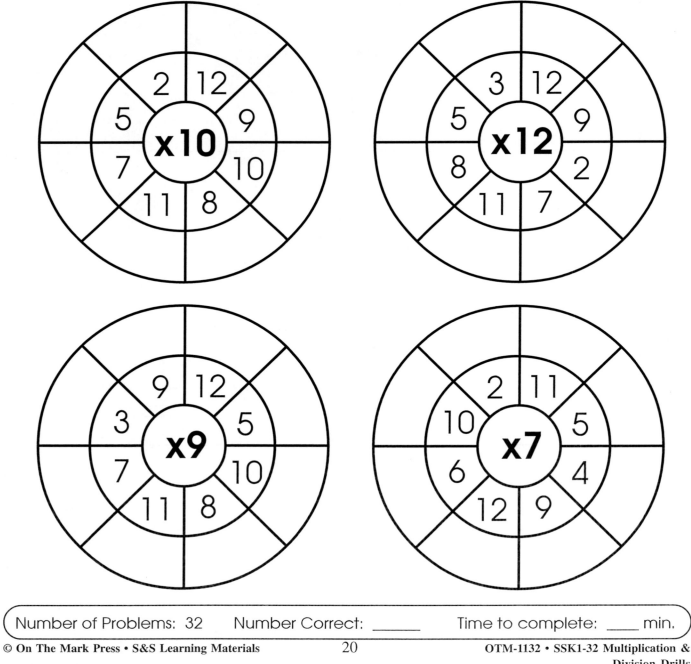

Number of Problems: 32   Number Correct: _____   Time to complete: ____ min.

Name: _____

Single Digit Multiplication

2 x 5	11 x 7	8 x 2	9 x 8	9 x 6
7 x 2	8 x 7	4 x 9	9 x 7	5 x 7
4 x 9	11 x 6	5 x 8	4 x 5	8 x 7
6 x 3	7 x 9	9 x 4	8 x 4	4 x 2
9 x 5	3 x 5	6 x 8	6 x 2	3 x 1
5 x 5	2 x 4	3 x 9	3 x 7	9 x 2

Number of Problems: 30   Number Correct: _____   Time to complete: _____ min.

Name: _____

Skill:
Single Digit Multiplication
No Regrouping

14 x 2	24 x 2	12 x 4	43 x 2	11 x 5
22 x 4	44 x 2	34 x 2	23 x 3	33 x 3
12 x 1	13 x 3	40 x 2	55 x 1	31 x 3
32 x 3	21 x 4	14 x 2	24 x 1	22 x 3
23 x 2	30 x 3	13 x 2	20 x 3	31 x 2
20 x 4	33 x 2	40 x 2	34 x 2	41 x 2

Number of Problems: 30   Number Correct: _____   Time to complete: ____ min.

Name: _____

Single Digit Multiplication

With Regrouping   No Regrouping

89	23	7	70	3
x 9	x 7	x 9	x 6	x 2

6	90	9	49	7
x 5	x 7	x 5	x 4	x 1

50	30	8	76	8
x 3	x 9	x 9	x 8	x 2

24	18	9	59	6
x 6	x 6	x 2	x 5	x 4

48	18	8	52	53
x 3	x 2	x 6	x 9	x 5

2	56	2	3	78
x 2	x 3	x 1	x 7	x 3

Number of Problems: 30   Number Correct: _____   Time to complete: ____ min.

Name: _____

Skill:

Rocket Ship Multiplication

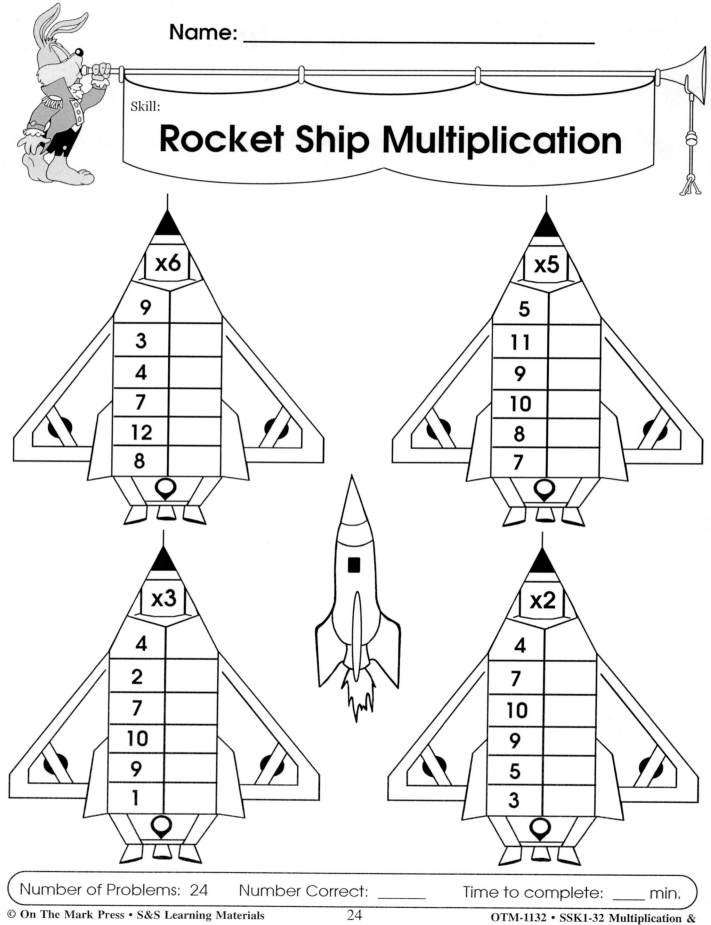

x6
9
3
4
7
12
8

x5
5
11
9
10
8
7

x3
4
2
7
10
9
1

x2
4
7
10
9
5
3

Number of Problems: 24   Number Correct: _____   Time to complete: ____ min.

OTM-1132 • SSK1-32 Multiplication & Division Drills

Name: _____

Single Digit Multiplication

Skill:

With Regrouping   No Regrouping

74	56	66	32	55
x 2	x 5	x 1	x 2	x 7

23	42	66	16	61
x 3	x 3	x 4	x 7	x 6

41	34	18	69	14
x 8	x 3	x 8	x 4	x 3

24	83	25	63	31
x 7	x 7	x 2	x 8	x 7

73	56	26	24	59
x 5	x 8	x 3	x 9	x 9

21	27	73	99	53
x 2	x 3	x 5	x 2	x 9

Number of Problems: 30   Number Correct: _____   Time to complete: ____ min.

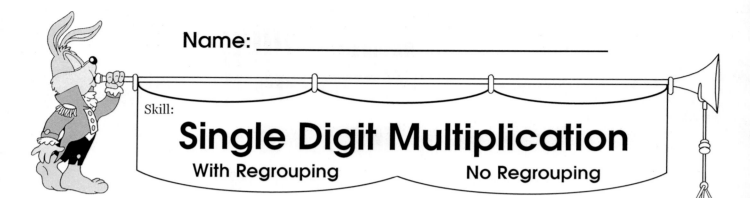

Skill:
Single Digit Multiplication
With Regrouping   No Regrouping

73 x 5 = ____   99 x 2 = ____   60 x 1 = ____

53 x 9 = ____   13 x 4 = ____   40 x 6 = ____

16 x 2 = ____   28 x 3 = ____   75 x 2 = ____

84 x 3 = ____   14 x 6 = ____   92 x 4 = ____

19 x 9 = ____   24 x 6 = ____   74 x 2 = ____

23 x 3 = ____   41 x 8 = ____   24 x 7 = ____

77 x 5 = ____   21 x 2 = ____   56 x 5 = ____

32 x 2 = ____   44 x 7 = ____   42 x 3 = ____

66 x 4 = ____   16 x 7 = ____   61 x 6 = ____

38 x 5 = ____   34 x 3 = ____   18 x 8 = ____

70 x 5 = ____   83 x 7 = ____   25 x 2 = ____

Number of Problems: 33   Number Correct: _____   Time to complete: ____ min.

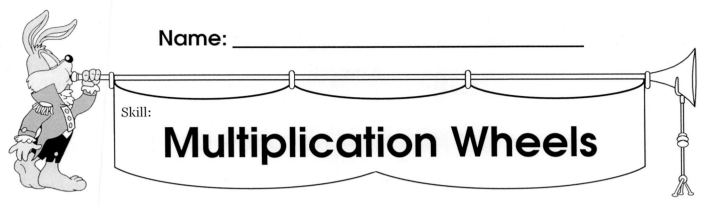

Name: _____

Skill:

Multiplication Wheels

Multiply the number in the middle with each number in turn. Then write your answer in the blank.

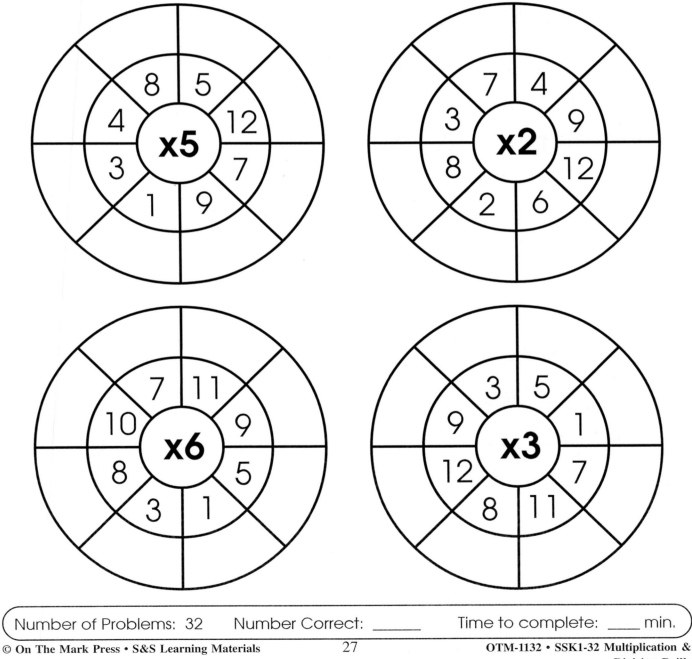

Number of Problems: 32   Number Correct: _____   Time to complete: ____ min.

© On The Mark Press • S&S Learning Materials   27   OTM-1132 • SSK1-32 Multiplication & Division Drills

Name: _____

Float the Boats

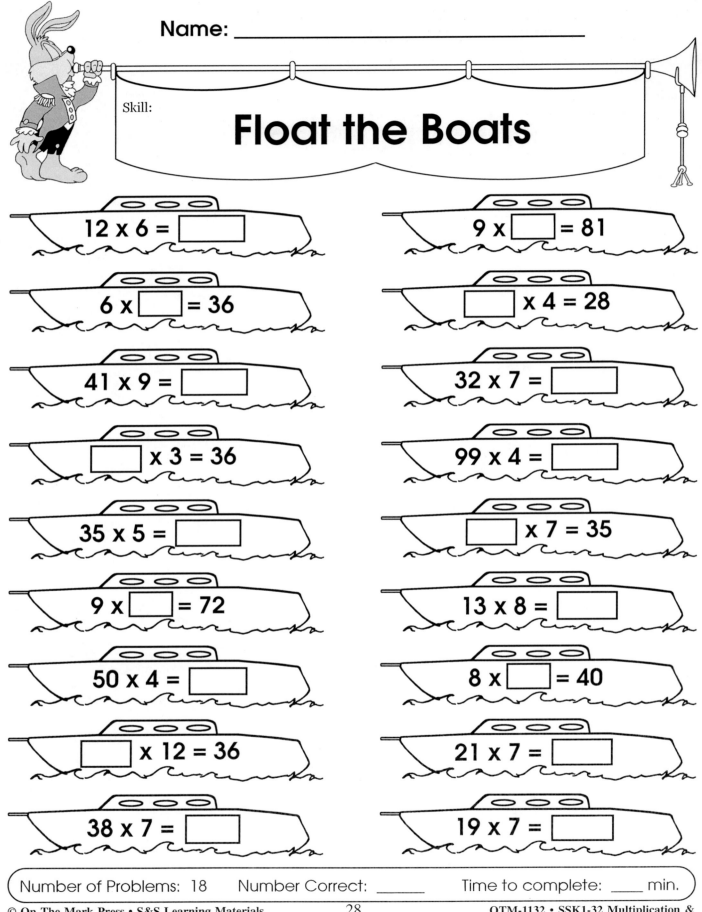

12 x 6 = ☐

6 x ☐ = 36

41 x 9 = ☐

☐ x 3 = 36

35 x 5 = ☐

9 x ☐ = 72

50 x 4 = ☐

☐ x 12 = 36

38 x 7 = ☐

9 x ☐ = 81

☐ x 4 = 28

32 x 7 = ☐

99 x 4 = ☐

☐ x 7 = 35

13 x 8 = ☐

8 x ☐ = 40

21 x 7 = ☐

19 x 7 = ☐

Number of Problems: 18   Number Correct: _____   Time to complete: ____ min.

Name: _____

Word Problems

Katie looked in her backyard to find the number of birds that were nesting. She found seven nests. If each nest is home to two adult birds, how many birds are nesting in Katie's backyard?

_____ X _____ = _____

Our football game was out of town and lots of fans wanted to go. Six buses with 84 people on each bus went to the game. How many fans went to the out of town game?

_____ X _____ = _____

Every Saturday afternoon, the movie theater sells out of popcorn. Every hour, they sell 225 bags. They are open for 3 hours. How many bags of popcorn do they sell all together?

_____ X _____ = _____

Sarah and Tiffany made candy apples for the Fun Fair. They made 17 dozen candy apples. How many apples are there?

_____ X _____ = _____

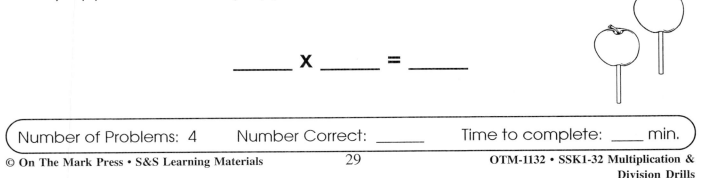

Number of Problems: 4   Number Correct: _____   Time to complete: _____ min.

Single Digit Multiplication

Skill:

With Regrouping

78 x 6	68 x 3	84 x 4	88 x 3
16 x 4	95 x 9	64 x 5	28 x 6
36 x 8	54 x 3	42 x 5	55 x 5
82 x 9	37 x 7	88 x 9	78 x 9
72 x 6	87 x 8	39 x 2	36 x 8
45 x 8	48 x 6	93 x 6	29 x 6
75 x 9	85 x 4	95 x 8	66 x 7

Number of Problems: 28   Number Correct: _____   Time to complete: ____ min.

Name: _____

More Rocket Ship Multiplication

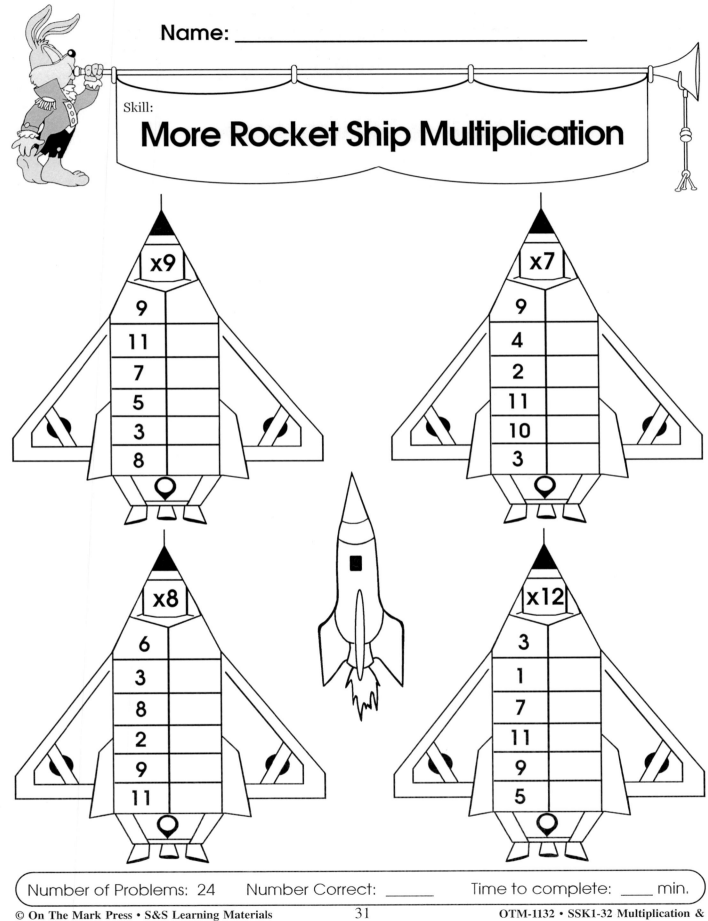

x9

9
11
7
5
3
8

x7

9
4
2
11
10
3

x8

6
3
8
2
9
11

x12

3
1
7
11
9
5

Number of Problems: 24   Number Correct: _____   Time to complete: ____ min.

Name: _____

Single Digit Multiplication

With Regrouping   No Regrouping

61	79	81	54
x 4	x 2	x 5	x 2

82	37	16	29
x 4	x 6	x 9	x 9

26	16	11	25
x 7	x 8	x 8	x 9

87	36	15	12
x 8	x 2	x 9	x 2

25	44	69	81
x 3	x 5	x 4	x 6

18	47	10	85
x 2	x 4	x 7	x 8

71	19	14	56
x 1	x 8	x 4	x 7

Number of Problems: 28   Number Correct: _____   Time to complete: ____ min.

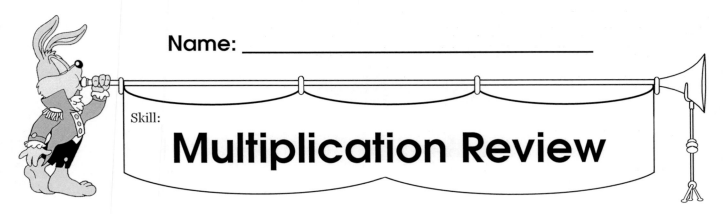

Name: _____

Multiplication Review

4 x 3 = _____   9 x 7 = _____   2 x 1 = _____

3 x 17 = _____   51 x 2 = _____   21 x 4 = _____

19 x 1 = _____   11 x 11 = _____   14 x 2 = _____

50 x 5 = _____   99 x 2 = _____   13 x 4 = _____

17 x 8 = _____   25 x 7 = _____   88 x 2 = _____

12 x 3 = _____   5 x 3 = _____   7 x 7 = _____

12 x 4 = _____   10 x 6 = _____   9 x 9 = _____

6 x 6 = _____   15 x 3 = _____   10 x 10 = _____

20 x 6 = _____   17 x 4 = _____   54 x 2 = _____

14 x 6 = _____   7 x 3 = _____   26 x 3 = _____

8 x 0 = _____   18 x 4 = _____   6 x 2 = _____

Number of Problems: 33   Number Correct: _____   Time to complete: ____ min.

Skill:

Two Digit Multiplication

38 x 37	42 x 23	77 x 41	45 x 12	35 x 21
44 x 36	38 x 18	20 x 17	77 x 56	65 x 58
12 x 11	32 x 27	94 x 90	28 x 25	89 x 11
87 x 19	22 x 16	16 x 15	54 x 10	90 x 55
94 x 48	34 x 34	98 x 80	21 x 15	81 x 57
79 x 58	94 x 18	52 x 48	22 x 18	89 x 87

Number of Problems: 30   Number Correct: _____   Time to complete: _____ min.

Name: _____

Skill:

Word Problems

In the auditorium, there are 27 rows of seats with 45 seats in each row. How many people can the auditorium seat?

_____ X _____ = _____

For the barbecue, Sandy bought 56 packages of rolls with 12 rolls in each package. How many rolls are there?

_____ X _____ = _____

Elizabeth and her sister moved into an apartment building that is 16 stories high. Each floor has 12 apartments. How many apartments are there all together?

_____ X _____ = _____

Jack has a part time job delivering newspapers. He earns $23.00 each week. How much money does he earn in one year?

_____ X _____ = _____

Number of Problems: 4   Number Correct: _____   Time to complete: ____ min.

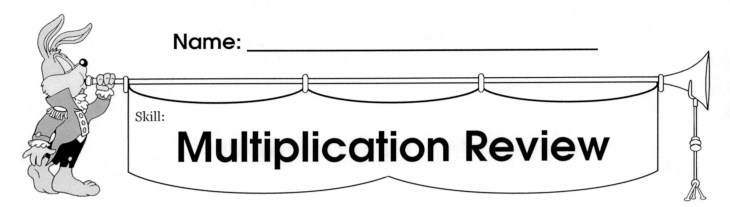

Skill:

Multiplication Review

62 x 5 = _____   51 x 3 = _____   54 x 6 = _____

94 x 8 = _____   35 x 7 = _____   60 x 9 = _____

33 x 3 = _____   79 x 6 = _____   27 x 4 = _____

33 x 7 = _____   71 x 2 = _____   12 x 3 = _____

79 x 2 = _____   26 x 7 = _____   63 x 4 = _____

40 x 4 = _____   48 x 1 = _____   85 x 7 = _____

56 x 3 = _____   85 x 8 = _____   88 x 8 = _____

36 x 9 = _____   16 x 8 = _____   36 x 2 = _____

46 x 4 = _____   87 x 8 = _____   57 x 5 = _____

20 x 4 = _____   66 x 5 = _____   65 x 2 = _____

44 x 5 = _____   56 x 9 = _____   53 x 2 = _____

92 x 4 = _____   43 x 8 = _____   50 x 9 = _____

Number of Problems: 36   Number Correct: _____   Time to complete: ____ min.

Name: _____

Skill: _____

You're a Star

11 x 3	20 x 6	27 x 6
52 x 7	17 x 6	17 x 17
29 x 6	27 x 5	62 x 9
11 x 11	40 x 17	26 x 19
78 x 17	72 x 24	57 x 37

Number of Problems: 15   Number Correct: _____   Time to complete: ____ min.

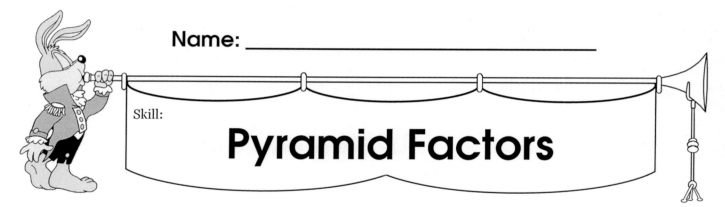

Name: _____

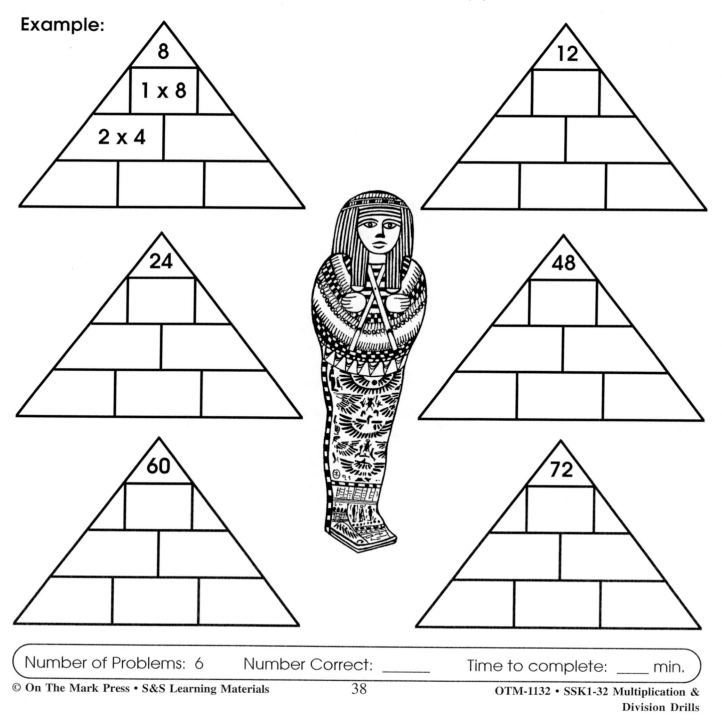

Skill:

Pyramid Factors

Look at the example below. Complete the other pyramid factors.

Example:

8
1 x 8
2 x 4

12

24

48

60

72

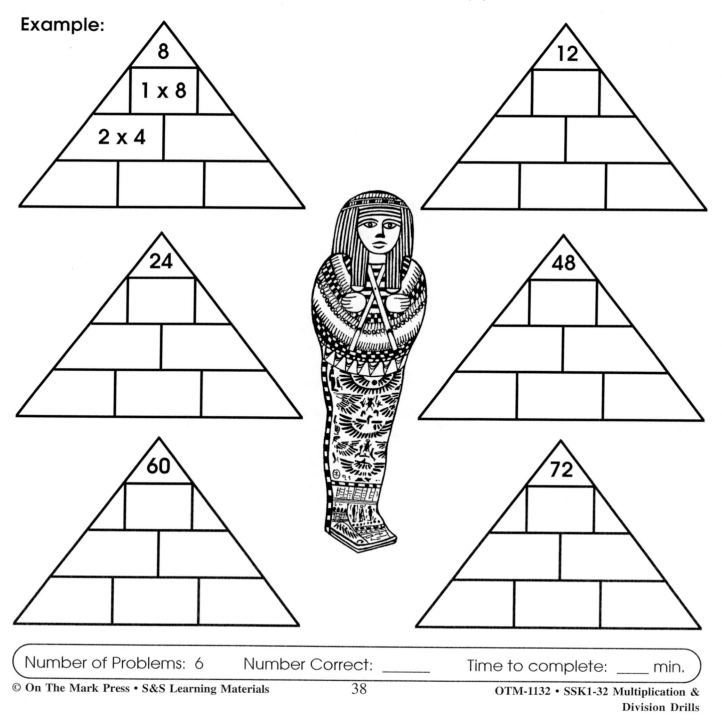

Number of Problems: 6   Number Correct: _____   Time to complete: ____ min.

© On The Mark Press • S&S Learning Materials   38   OTM-1132 • SSK1-32 Multiplication &
                                                                                        Division Drills

Skill:

Two Digit Multiplication

With Regrouping

38 x 21	46 x 12	51 x 19	87 x 23	19 x 11
76 x 25	28 x 17	32 x 24	81 x 56	56 x 37
67 x 33	75 x 69	84 x 56	97 x 88	61 x 59
95 x 17	77 x 39	86 x 47	93 x 54	29 x 19
23 x 18	48 x 27	78 x 34	85 x 83	68 x 56

Number of Problems: 25   Number Correct: _____   Time to complete: ____ min.

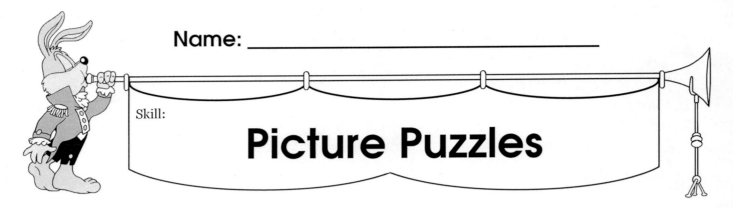

Name: _____

Skill: _____

Picture Puzzles

Joey is buying 6 ⚾. Each ball costs $2.75. How much will the total cost be?

_____

Taylor plays golf every summer. He buys 6 boxes of 🏌. Each box costs $13.79. How much does he spend on golf balls?

_____

Samantha and Trish made 🍪 for the bake sale. They made 27 dozen and sold each dozen for $1.50. How much money did they make?

_____

The students in Mr. Waters' class had a 🍕 party. They ordered 9 🍕. Each one cost $12.79. How much did the pizza cost all together?

_____

Number of Problems: 4   Number Correct: _____   Time to complete: _____ min.

Name: _____

Even More Rocket Ship Multiplication

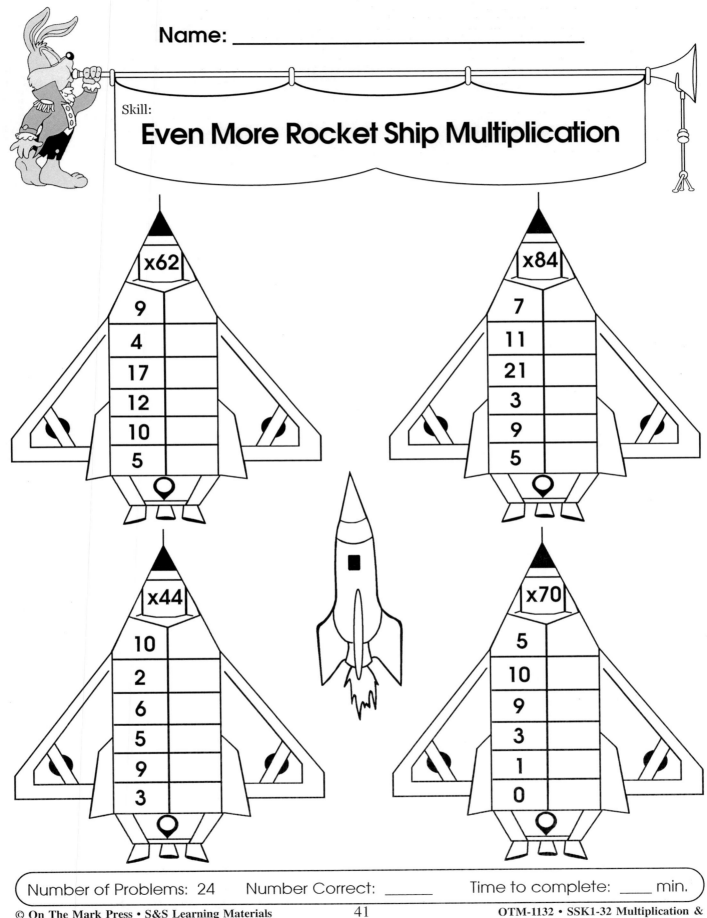

x62
9
4
17
12
10
5

x84
7
11
21
3
9
5

x44
10
2
6
5
9
3

x70
5
10
9
3
1
0

Number of Problems: 24   Number Correct: _____   Time to complete: ____ min.

Name: _____

Skill:
Balloon Multiplication

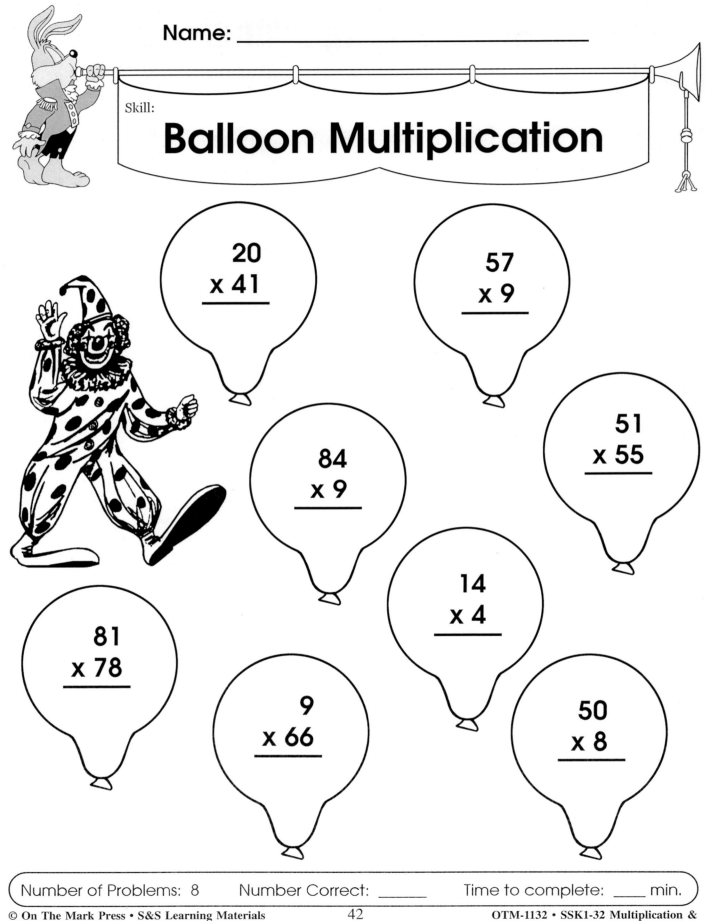

20
x 41
____

57
x 9
____

84
x 9
____

51
x 55
____

14
x 4
____

81
x 78
____

9
x 66
____

50
x 8
____

Number of Problems: 8   Number Correct: _____   Time to complete: ____ min.

Name: _____

Skill:

Word Problems

Kendra is buying new clothes for her vacation. She has decided to buy 4 sets of shorts with a matching top. Each short set is $14.98. How much will 4 sets cost?

_____ X _____ = _____

Ken is the photographer for the school football team. At each game, he takes 63 pictures. How many pictures will he take if he goes to 17 games?

_____ X _____ = _____

Mary and Peter have opened a lemonade stand for the summer. They are selling a glass of lemonade for 25¢. On their first day, they sold 216 glasses of lemonade. How much money did they make?

_____ X _____ = _____

Rhonda is baby-sitting for 5 hours every day during the month of July. How many hours will she baby-sit?

_____ X _____ = _____

Number of Problems: 4   Number Correct: _____   Time to complete: _____ min.

Name: _____

Bubble Multiplication

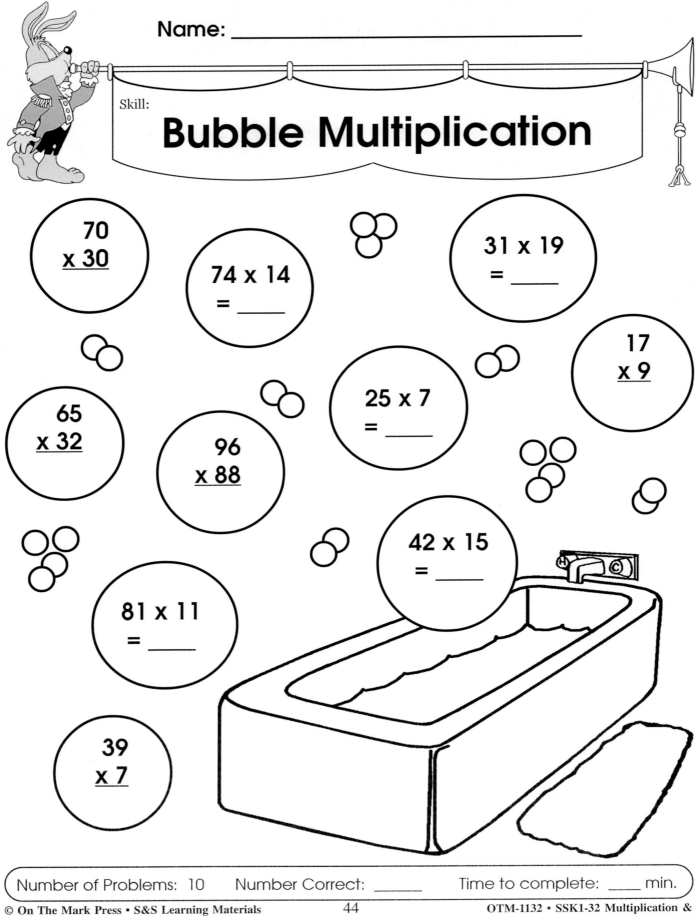

70
x 30

74 x 14
= _____

31 x 19
= _____

17
x 9

65
x 32

96
x 88

25 x 7
= _____

42 x 15
= _____

81 x 11
= _____

39
x 7

Number of Problems: 10   Number Correct: _____   Time to complete: ____ min.

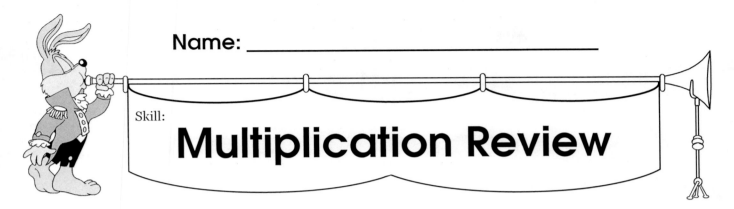

Skill: Multiplication Review

36 x 23 = ____	84 x 13 = ____	54 x 17 = ____
51 x 35 = ____	40 x 37 = ____	94 x 28 = ____
88 x 16 = ____	79 x 11 = ____	12 x 10 = ____
35 x 18 = ____	57 x 51 = ____	83 x 32 = ____
60 x 59 = ____	32 x 31 = ____	33 x 13 = ____
66 x 15 = ____	76 x 52 = ____	35 x 19 = ____
79 x 76 = ____	65 x 52 = ____	72 x 65 = ____
27 x 14 = ____	37 x 24 = ____	92 x 22 = ____
56 x 14 = ____	37 x 10 = ____	27 x 19 = ____
33 x 24 = ____	53 x 21 = ____	87 x 18 = ____
92 x 41 = ____	90 x 44 = ____	50 x 39 = ____

Number of Problems: 33   Number Correct: _____   Time to complete: ____ min.

Name: _____

Skill:

Lunch Bag Multiplication

Write three different number sentences that will give you the correct answer.

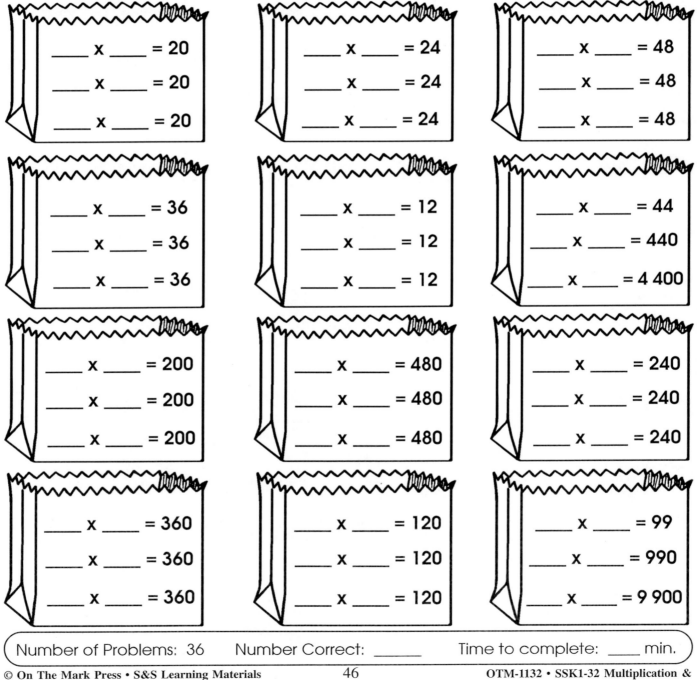

____ x ____ = 20
____ x ____ = 20
____ x ____ = 20

____ x ____ = 24
____ x ____ = 24
____ x ____ = 24

____ x ____ = 48
____ x ____ = 48
____ x ____ = 48

____ x ____ = 36
____ x ____ = 36
____ x ____ = 36

____ x ____ = 12
____ x ____ = 12
____ x ____ = 12

____ x ____ = 44
____ x ____ = 440
____ x ____ = 4 400

____ x ____ = 200
____ x ____ = 200
____ x ____ = 200

____ x ____ = 480
____ x ____ = 480
____ x ____ = 480

____ x ____ = 240
____ x ____ = 240
____ x ____ = 240

____ x ____ = 360
____ x ____ = 360
____ x ____ = 360

____ x ____ = 120
____ x ____ = 120
____ x ____ = 120

____ x ____ = 99
____ x ____ = 990
____ x ____ = 9 900

Number of Problems: 36   Number Correct: _____   Time to complete: ____ min.

Skill: _____

Two Digit Multiplication

2277 x 82	8858 x 53	8912 x 76	4402 x 31
2025 x 55	9005 x 24	842 x 35	186 x 14
989 x 39	5898 x 87	8564 x 78	7541 x 63
668 x 47	9712 x 29	8984 x 72	2613 x 36
8994 x 65	769 x 4	576 x 93	7182 x 92

Number of Problems: 20   Number Correct: _____   Time to complete: ____ min.

Name: _____

Skill:

Banner Multiplication

19	27	74	37
x 8	x 6	x 3	x 6

67	69	32	46
x 85	x 27	x 49	x 79

499	769	342	648
x 21	x 42	x 33	x 32

476	367	460	448
x 276	x 694	x 126	x 749

Number of Problems: 16   Number Correct: _____   Time to complete: ____ min.

Skill:

Three Digit Multiplication

837	765	261	869
x 117	x 731	x 103	x 707

603	738	961	835
x 346	x 548	x 118	x 550

441	981	820	850
x 137	x 230	x 309	x 805

596	771	491	446
x 214	x 570	x 125	x 342

711	557	985	421
x 306	x 371	x 538	x 390

Number of Problems: 20   Number Correct: _____   Time to complete: ____ min.

Skill:

Multiplication Review
With Two and Three Digit Numbers

245 x 24	297 x 19	622 x 681	2649 x 292
81 x 39	8029 x 732	2742 x 359	7432 x 947
5248 x 823	7098 x 817	837 x 59	642 x 37
94 x 68	125 x 79	336 x 66	479 x 237
693 x 27	2612 x 268	9462 x 292	7422 x 359

Number of Problems: 20   Number Correct: _____   Time to complete: ____ min.

Skill: _____

Three Digit Multiplication

4949 x 342	1396 x 270	4788 x 136	769 x 176
2384 x 222	123 x 104	633 x 166	2001 x 403
2374 x 332	5469 x 439	9224 x 536	470 x 327
3447 x 985	1826 x 118	3524 x 189	3314 x 580
7377 x 602	771 x 720	700 x 205	2208 x 207

Number of Problems: 20   Number Correct: _____   Time to complete: ____ min.

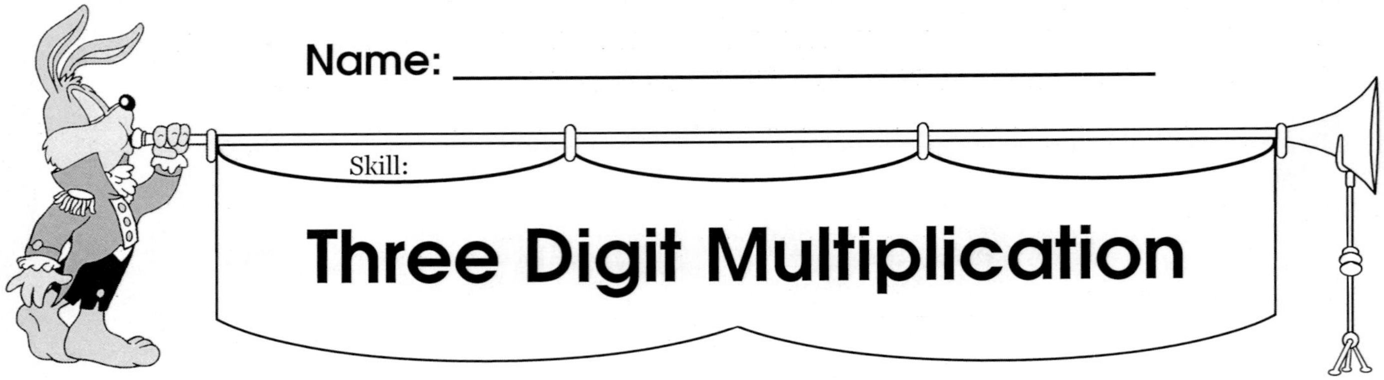

Skill:

Three Digit Multiplication

8802 x 435	9111 x 719	8210 x 480	7495 x 265
5947 x 956	8105 x 702	252 x 167	3851 x 885
197 x 242	5620 x 219	4491 x 445	125 x 179
5018 x 207	594 x 299	346 x 197	8909 x 600
742 x 970	8515 x 285	2684 x 135	2218 x 117

Number of Problems: 20   Number Correct: _____   Time to complete: ____ min.

Word Problems

Skill:

Mrs. Jones wanted to estimate the number of books in the library. There were 276 shelves and on one shelf there were 38 books. How many books did she estimate were in the library?

_____ X _____ = _____

A ticket to the movie is $5.75. One evening 347 people went to the movie. How much money was made that evening?

_____ X _____ = _____

Nicole has been saving her allowance for three years. She has made 212 deposits. Each time she has deposited $27.25. How much money has she deposited to her savings account?

_____ X _____ = _____

The paper factory makes 64 756 packages of paper each day. How many packages of paper will the factory make in 30 days?

_____ X _____ = _____

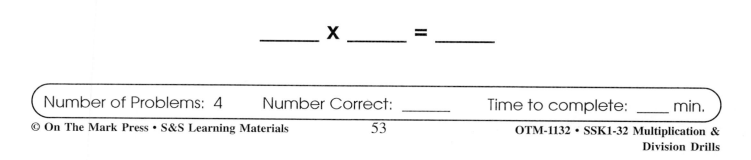

Number of Problems: 4   Number Correct: _____   Time to complete: _____ min.

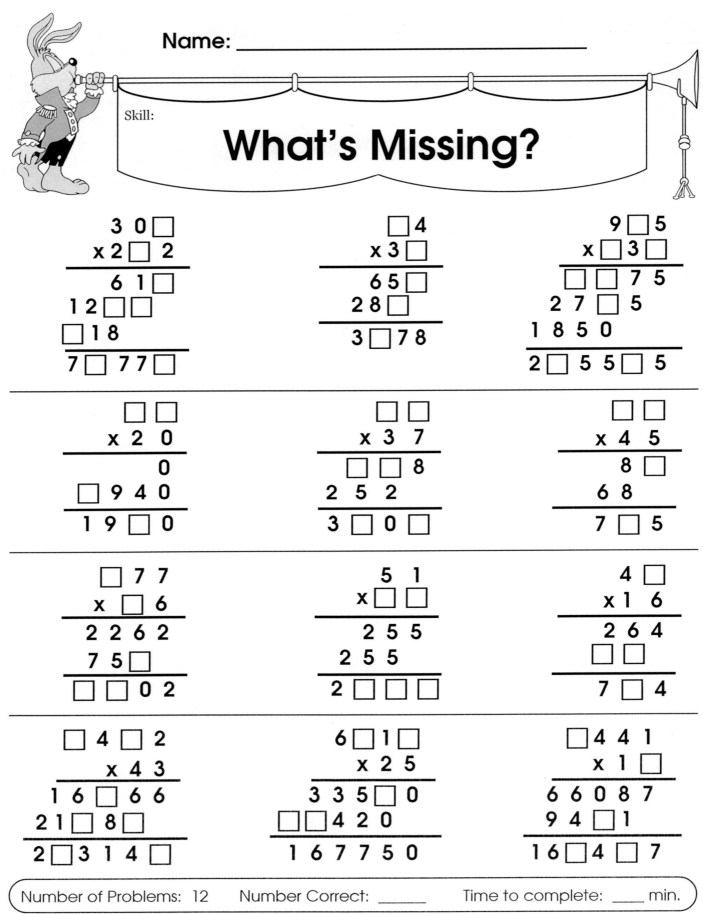

Name: _____

Skill: _____

What's Missing?

Problem 1
```
    3 0 □
  x 2 □ 2
  ─────────
    6 1 □
  1 2 □ □
  □ 1 8
  ─────────
  7 □ 7 7 □
```

Problem 2
```
    □ 4
  x 3 □
  ───────
  6 5 □
  2 8 □
  ───────
  3 □ 7 8
```

Problem 3
```
    9 □ 5
  x □ 3 □
  ───────────
  □ □ 7 5
  2 7 □ 5
  1 8 5 0
  ───────────
  2 □ 5 5 □ 5
```

Problem 4
```
    □ □
  x 2 0
  ───────
      0
  □ 9 4 0
  ───────
  1 9 □ 0
```

Problem 5
```
    □ □
  x 3 7
  ───────
  □ □ 8
  2 5 2
  ───────
  3 □ 0 □
```

Problem 6
```
    □ □
  x 4 5
  ───────
    8 □
  6 8
  ───────
  7 □ 5
```

Problem 7
```
    □ 7 7
  x   □ 6
  ─────────
  2 2 6 2
  7 5 □
  ─────────
  □ □ 0 2
```

Problem 8
```
    5 1
  x □ □
  ───────
  2 5 5
  2 5 5
  ───────
  2 □ □ □
```

Problem 9
```
    4 □
  x 1 6
  ───────
  2 6 4
  □ □
  ───────
  7 □ 4
```

Problem 10
```
    □ 4 □ 2
  x     4 3
  ───────────
  1 6 □ 6 6
  2 1 □ 8 □
  ───────────
  2 □ 3 1 4 □
```

Problem 11
```
    6 □ 1 □
  x     2 5
  ───────────
  3 3 5 □ 0
  □ □ 4 2 0
  ───────────
  1 6 7 7 5 0
```

Problem 12
```
    □ 4 4 1
  x     1 □
  ───────────
  6 6 0 8 7
  9 4 □ 1
  ───────────
  1 6 □ 4 □ 7
```

Number of Problems: 12   Number Correct: _____   Time to complete: ____ min.

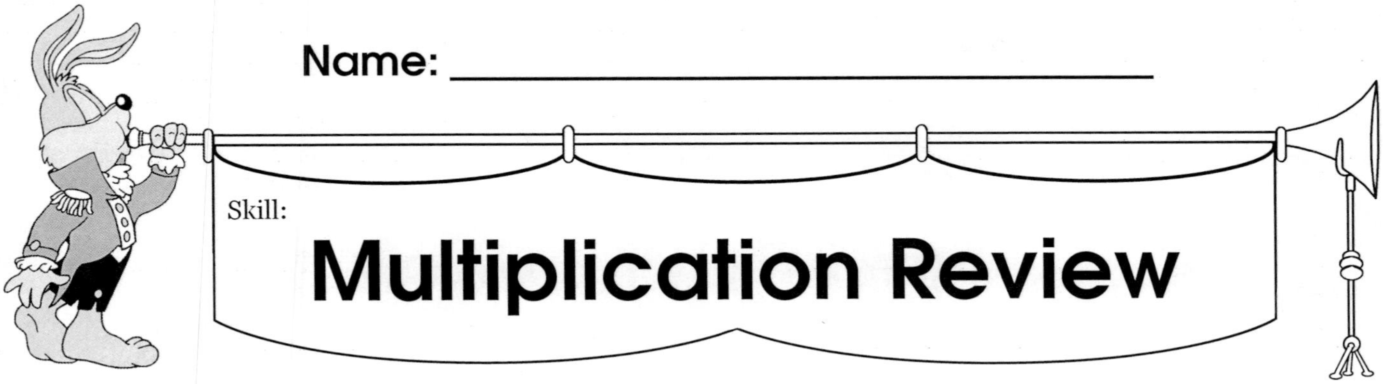

Skill:

Multiplication Review

4116	3378	7488
x 3766	x 2280	x 4904

8989	5850	2961
x 8457	x 504	x 1278

7814	8997	6296
x 7709	x 133	x 2989

3571	2845	1373
x 341	x 378	x 649

1343	8662	5255
x 1146	x 1512	x 362

Number of Problems: 15   Number Correct: _____   Time to complete: ____ min.

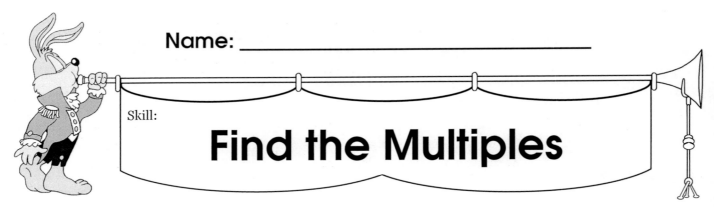

Name: _____

Skill:

Find the Multiples

Shade in the multiples for each block.

9

11	18	36	20		12
16	32		45		9
81	54	43	63	90	
4	99	27	108		

7

9	14	64	42		58
13	84		21		77
39	18		35	90	
41	26	49	63		

3

11	6	17	33		30
27	42		21		51
36	19	62	16	25	
24	40	45			

11

24	30	57	64		12
22	54		55		77
33	43		121	11	
88	99	27	66		

8

27	72	57	16		22
24	5		48		88
32	97	8	81	80	
43	40	64	101	17	

5

25	21	5	19		10
32	65		45		26
15	64	40	50	48	
55	91	70	100		

Number of Problems: 6   Number Correct: _____   Time to complete: ____ min.

OTM-1132 • SSK1-32 Multiplication & Division Drills

Skill:

Multiplying Decimals

0.55 x 0.80	0.11 x 0.01	0.27 x 0.23	0.31 x 0.01
0.66 x 0.05	0.42 x 0.07	0.04 x 0.04	0.43 x 0.37
4.69 x 0.79	3.26 x 0.62	6.35 x 4.96	6.83 x 5.27
7.57 x 6.52	1.52 x 6.0	2.58 x 9.7	2.71 x 1.36
4.17 x 2.6	7.71 x 0.84	1.73 x 2.1	2.2 x 0.7
2.9 x 0.48	6.63 x 8.0	0.09 x 0.06	1.44 x .08

Number of Problems: 24   Number Correct: _____   Time to complete: ____ min.

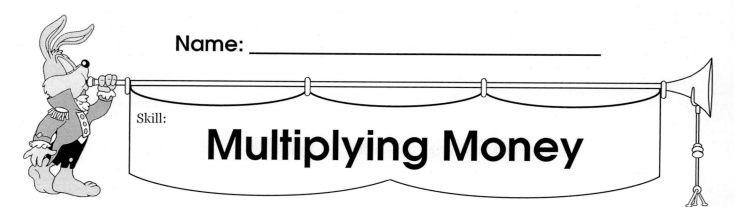

Skill:

Multiplying Money

$76.43
x   19

$421.27
x   34

$9.79
x 24

$36.59
x 214

$1.25
x 47

$62.99
x 401

$79.87
x   64

$39.97
x   78

$44.86
x 125

$33.01
x   99

$112.94
x   89

$92.64
x 521

$12.77
x 642

$32.32
x   47

$98.41
x   52

Number of Problems: 15   Number Correct: _____   Time to complete: ____ min.

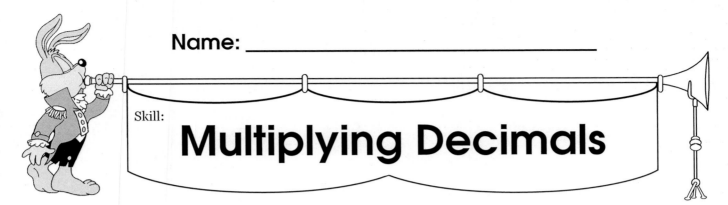

Skill:

Multiplying Decimals

83.09 x 4.84	84.81 x 32.04	93.29 x 4.35
66.97 x 31.24	32.1 x 1.8	59.01 x 36.69
75.91 x 42.95	14.72 x 8.84	18.18 x 4.83
72.55 x 18.20	24.42 x 7.42	20.19 x 0.41
94.74 x 80	11.55 x 0.09	24.67 x 2.42

Number of Problems: 15   Number Correct: _____   Time to complete: ____ min.

Two Methods for Mastering Long Division

1. Traditional "Bring Down" Method (with 1-Digit Divisor)

This procedure requires students to have memorized or be able to calculate the standard multiplication facts for factors 1 through 10. In this method, long division is broken down into a series of steps, each one calculating the number of times the divisor "goes into" each single digit of the multiple-digit dividend.

Example: $679 \div 5 = ?$

Begin by calculating the number of times the divisor (5) goes into the hundreds digit (6) of the dividend 679 [see calculation a)]. For each subsequent step, the next digit of the dividend is brought down, and the calculation is continued until the dividend has been reduced such that the divisor cannot be divided into it [calculations b), c) and d)].

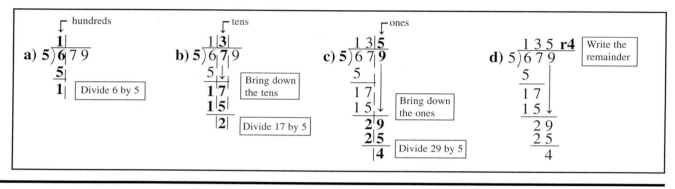

2. Modified Long Division Method (with 1-Digit Divisor)

This procedure allows students to solve a long division problem in smaller, more manageable steps than those required for the traditional method. This method is especially useful for students who are experiencing difficulty memorizing or calculating all of the multiplication facts from 1 through 10 as **only the multiplication facts for factors 1, 2, 5 and 10 are required**. Each step in the modified method calculates the number of times (either 10, 5, 2 or 1) the divisor goes into the multiple-digit dividend.

Example: $132 \div 7 = ?$

Begin by calculating the number of times the divisor (7) goes into the dividend 132 using only a factor or 10, 5, 2 or 1 (i.e., 7 goes into 132 a total of 10 times since 10 x 7=70). Then, subtract 70 from the dividend (132-70= 62) [see calculation a)]. Continue the calculation until the dividend has been reduced such that the divisor cannot be divided into it [calculations b), c) and d)]. Complete the problem by finding the sum of all the factors used in the calculations (10+5+2+1=18) [calculation e)].

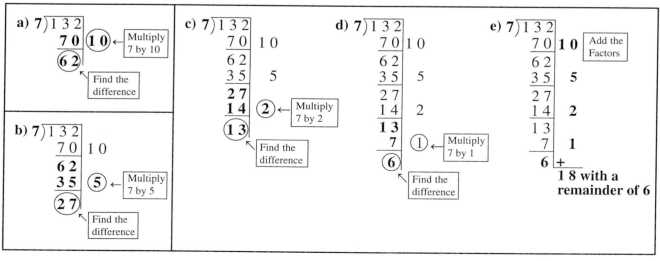

Division
Drill
Work Sheets

Name: _____

Skill:

Picture Division

Write a division fact for each picture.

Divide 8 cacti into groups of 4.

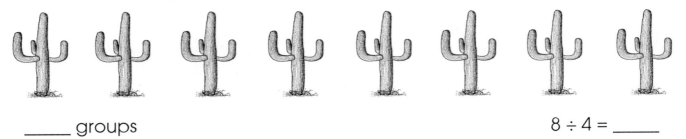

_____ groups   8 ÷ 4 = _____

Divide 12 basses into groups of 3.

_____ groups   12 ÷ 3 = _____

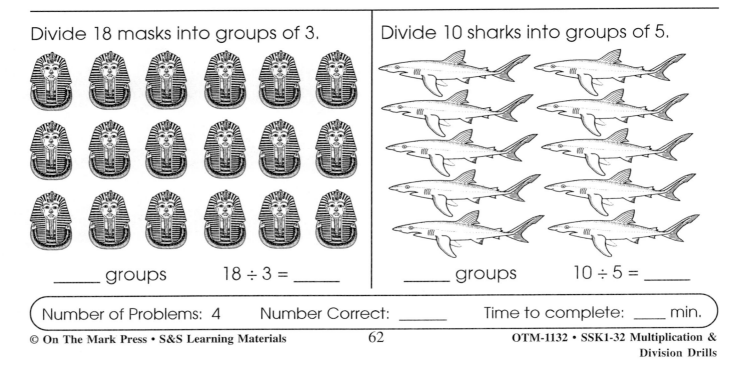

Divide 18 masks into groups of 3.

_____ groups   18 ÷ 3 = _____

Divide 10 sharks into groups of 5.

_____ groups   10 ÷ 5 = _____

Number of Problems: 4   Number Correct: _____   Time to complete: _____ min.

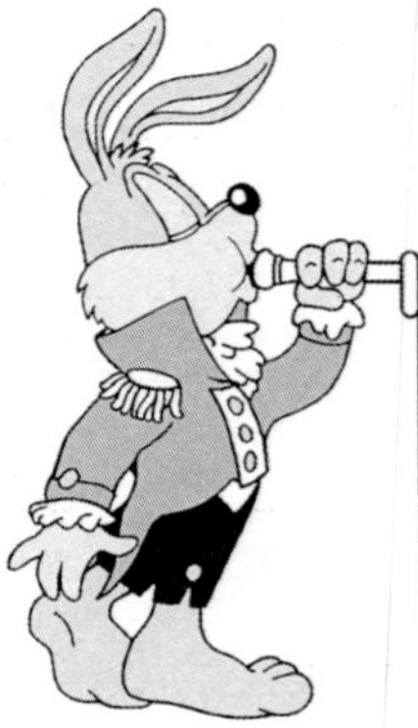

Name: ______________________________

Skill:

Division ÷1

$\begin{array}{r}5\\1\overline{)}\end{array}$	$1\overline{)9}$	$1\overline{)1}$	$\begin{array}{r}6\\1\overline{)}\end{array}$	$1\overline{)2}$
$1\overline{)0}$	$\begin{array}{r}7\\1\overline{)}\end{array}$	$1\overline{)8}$	$1\overline{)4}$	$1\overline{)3}$
$1\overline{)7}$	$\begin{array}{r}9\\1\overline{)}\end{array}$	$1\overline{)5}$	$\begin{array}{r}8\\1\overline{)}\end{array}$	$1\overline{)6}$

6 ÷ 1 = ____	3 ÷ 1 = ____	____ ÷ 1 = 9
0 ÷ 1 = ____	8 ÷ 1 = ____	2 ÷ 1 = ____
____ ÷ 1 = 5	4 ÷ 1 = ____	7 ÷ 1 = ____
1 ÷ 1 = ____	9 ÷ 1 = ____	____ ÷ 1 = 0
____ ÷ 1 = 6	5 ÷ 1 = ____	____ ÷ 1 = 2

Number of Problems: 30 Number Correct: _____ Time to complete: ____ min.

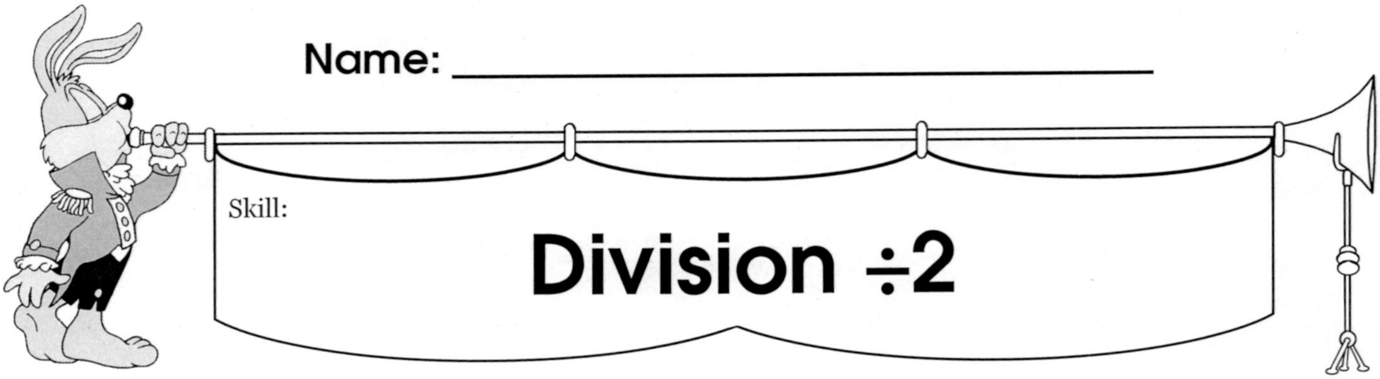

Skill:

Division ÷2

$$2\overline{)6} \qquad 2\overline{)2} \qquad 2\overline{)10} \qquad 2\overline{)}^{\,3} \qquad 2\overline{)16}$$

$$2\overline{)12} \qquad 2\overline{)}^{\,9} \qquad 2\overline{)2} \qquad 2\overline{)}^{\,5} \qquad 2\overline{)}^{\,12}$$

$2 + 2 + 2 + 2 + 2 + 2 =$ _____

_____ groups of the number _____   _____ $\div 2 = 6$

$4 \div 2 =$ _____ $10 \div 2 =$ _____

_____ $\div 2 = 6$ $2 \div$ _____ $= 1$

$18 \div 2 =$ _____ $20 \div 2 =$ _____

$12 \div 2 =$ _____   _____ $\div 2 = 9$

_____ $\div 2 = 7$ $16 \div 2 =$ _____

$2 + 2 + 2 + 2 + 2 + 2 + 2 + 2 + 2 =$ _____

_____ groups of the number _____ $18 \div 2 =$ _____

Number of Problems: 22   Number Correct: _____   Time to complete: ____ min.

Name: _____

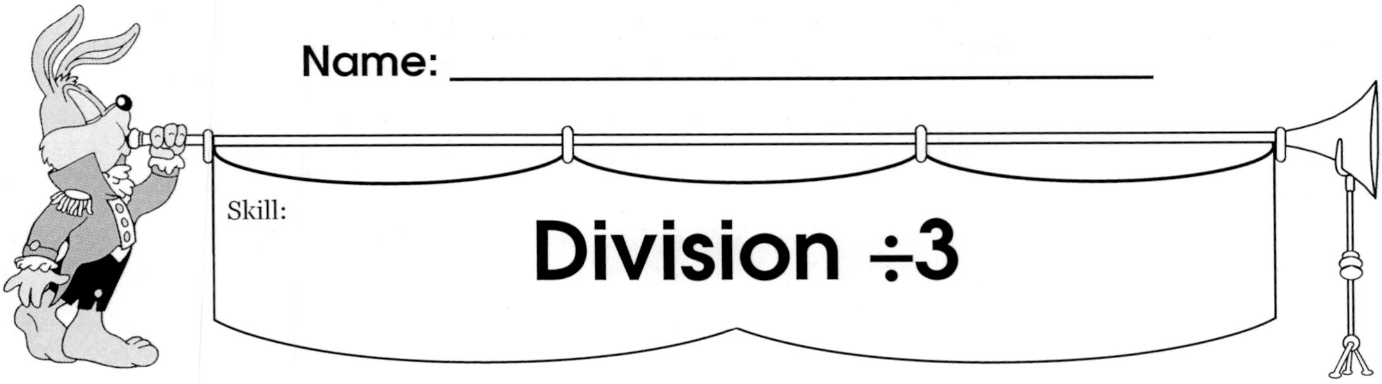

Skill: _____

Division ÷3

$$3\overline{)18} \qquad 3\overline{)9} \qquad 3\overline{)30} \qquad 3\overline{)}^{5} \qquad 3\overline{)27}$$

$$3\overline{)3} \qquad 3\overline{)15} \qquad 3\overline{)}^{6} \qquad 3\overline{)6} \qquad 3\overline{)}^{8}$$

3 + 3 + 3 + 3 + 3 = _____

_____ groups of the number _____   _____ ÷ 3 = 5

12 ÷ 3 = _____   9 ÷ 3 = _____

_____ ÷ 3 = 2   24 ÷ 3 = _____

30 ÷ 3 = _____   _____ ÷ 3 = 6

45 ÷ 3 = _____   15 ÷ 3 = _____

_____ ÷ 3 = 4   27 ÷ 3 = _____

3 + 3 + 3 + 3 + 3 + 3 + 3 + 3 + 3 + 3 = _____

_____ groups of the number _____   30 ÷ 3 = _____

Number of Problems: 22   Number Correct: _____   Time to complete: _____ min.

OTM-1132 • SSK1-32 Multiplication & Division Drills

Name: _____

Division ÷4

$4\overline{)12}$　　　$4\overline{)24}$　　　$4\overline{)4}$　　　$4\overset{3}{\overline{)}}$　　　$4\overline{)28}$

$4\overline{)32}$　　　$4\overline{)16}$　　　$4\overset{10}{\overline{)}}$　　　$4\overline{)36}$　　　$4\overline{)8}$

$4 + 4 + 4 + 4 + 4 + 4 + 4 =$ ____

____ groups of the number ____　　　　$28 \div 4 =$ ____

$16 \div 4 =$ ____　　　　　　____ $\div 4 = 1$

$32 \div 4 =$ ____　　　　　　____ $\div 4 = 3$

____ $\div 4 = 10$　　　　　　$32 \div 4 =$ ____

$12 \div 4 =$ ____　　　　　　$28 \div 4 =$ ____

____ $\div 4 = 9$　　　　　　$8 \div 4 =$ ____

$4 + 4 + 4 + 4 + 4 + 4 + 4 + 4 + 4 + 4 + 4 =$ ____

____ groups of the number ____　　　　____ $\div 4 = 11$

Number of Problems: 22　　Number Correct: _____　　Time to complete: ____ min.

Name: ______________________________

Skill:

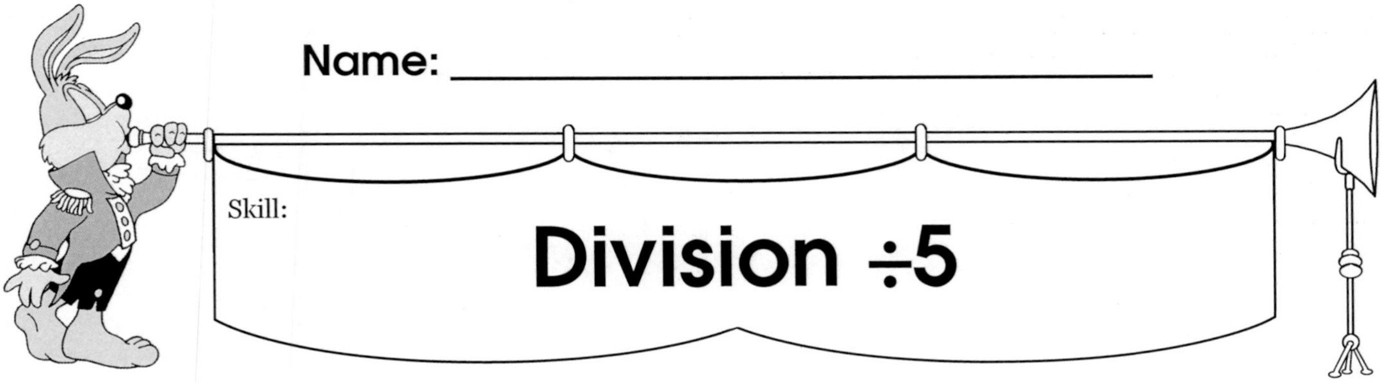

Division ÷5

$5\overline{)10}$ $\begin{array}{r}6\\5\overline{)\quad}\end{array}$ $5\overline{)50}$ $5\overline{)25}$ $5\overline{)40}$

$\begin{array}{r}3\\5\overline{)\quad}\end{array}$ $5\overline{)30}$ $\begin{array}{r}4\\5\overline{)\quad}\end{array}$ $5\overline{)5}$ $\begin{array}{r}7\\5\overline{)\quad}\end{array}$

---

5 + 5 + 5 + 5 + 5 + 5 + 5 + 5 + 5 = ____

____ groups of the number ____ ____ ÷ 5 = 9

---

35 ÷ 5 = ____ ____ ÷ 5 = 3

5 ÷ 5 = ____ 20 ÷ 5 = ____

55 ÷ 5 = ____ 25 ÷ 5 = ____

10 ÷ 5 = ____ 40 ÷ 5 = ____

____ ÷ 5 = 6 45 ÷ 5 = ____

---

5 + 5 + 5 + 5 + 5 + 5 + 5 + 5 + 5 + 5 + 5 + 5 = ____

____ groups of the number ____ 60 ÷ 5 = ____

Number of Problems: 22 Number Correct: ______ Time to complete: ____ min.

Skill: _____

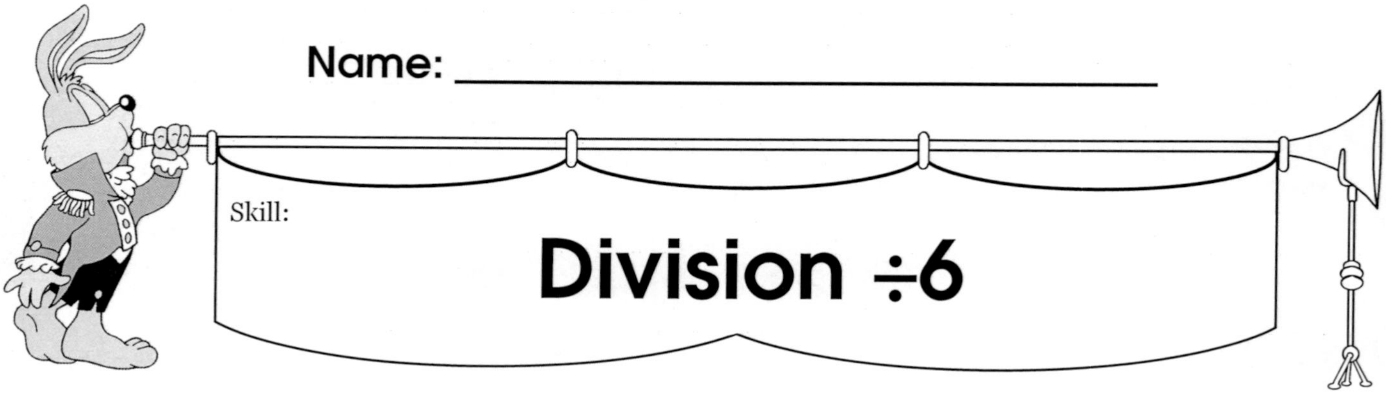

Division ÷6

$6\overline{)30}$ $6\overline{)}^{1}$ $6\overline{)42}$ $6\overline{)60}$ $6\overline{)}^{3}$

$6\overline{)}^{4}$ $6\overline{)12}$ $6\overline{)}^{8}$ $6\overline{)36}$ $6\overline{)54}$

$6 + 6 + 6 + 6 + 6 + 6 =$ ____

____ groups of the number ____ $36 \div 6 =$ ____

$36 \div 6 =$ ____ $48 \div 6 =$ ____

____ $\div 6 = 2$ $24 \div 6 =$ ____

____ $\div 6 = 9$ ____ $\div 6 = 7$

$30 \div 6 =$ ____ $6 \div 6 =$ ____

$60 \div 6 =$ ____ $18 \div 6 =$ ____

$6 + 6 + 6 + 6 + 6 + 6 + 6 + 6 + 6 + 6 =$ ____

____ groups of the number ____   ____ $\div 6 = 10$

Number of Problems: 22   Number Correct: _____   Time to complete: ____ min.

Skill:

Division ÷7

$$7\overline{)28} \qquad 7\overline{)}^{10} \qquad 7\overline{)14} \qquad 7\overline{)49} \qquad 7\overline{)21}$$

$$7\overline{)}^{1} \qquad 7\overline{)42} \qquad 7\overline{)}^{5} \qquad 7\overline{)63} \qquad 7\overline{)56}$$

7 + 7 + 7 + 7 + 7 + 7 + 7 + 7 + 7 = _____

_____ groups of the number _____   _____ ÷ 7 = 9

21 ÷ 7 = _____   35 ÷ 7 = _____

_____ ÷ 7 = 1   42 ÷ 7 = _____

_____ ÷ 7 = 8   _____ ÷ 7 = 9

49 ÷ 7 = _____   _____ ÷ 7 = 4

70 ÷ 7 = _____   14 ÷ 7 = _____

7 + 7 + 7 + 7 + 7 + 7 + 7 = _____

_____ groups of the number _____   49 ÷ 7 = _____

Number of Problems: 22   Number Correct: _____   Time to complete: ____ min.

© On The Mark Press • S&S Learning Materials   69   OTM-1132 • SSK1-32 Multiplication &
Division Drills

Name: ______________________________

Skill:
Division ÷8

$\begin{array}{r}3\\8\overline{)}\end{array}$ $8\overline{)8}$ $8\overline{)56}$ $8\overline{)32}$ $\begin{array}{r}8\\8\overline{)}\end{array}$

$8\overline{)16}$ $\begin{array}{r}5\\8\overline{)}\end{array}$ $\begin{array}{r}10\\8\overline{)}\end{array}$ $8\overline{)72}$ $8\overline{)48}$

---

8 + 8 + 8 + 8 = ____

____ groups of the number ____ ____ ÷ 8 = 4

____ ÷ 8 = 1 64 ÷ 8 = ____

16 ÷ 8 = ____ ____ ÷ 8 = 6

72 ÷ 8 = ____ 24 ÷ 8 = ____

____ ÷ 8 = 4 ____ ÷ 8 = 7

____ ÷ 8 = 10 40 ÷ 8 = ____

---

8 + 8 + 8 + 8 + 8 + 8 + 8 + 8 = ____

____ groups of the number ____ 64 ÷ 8 = ____

Number of Problems: 22 Number Correct: _____ Time to complete: ____ min.

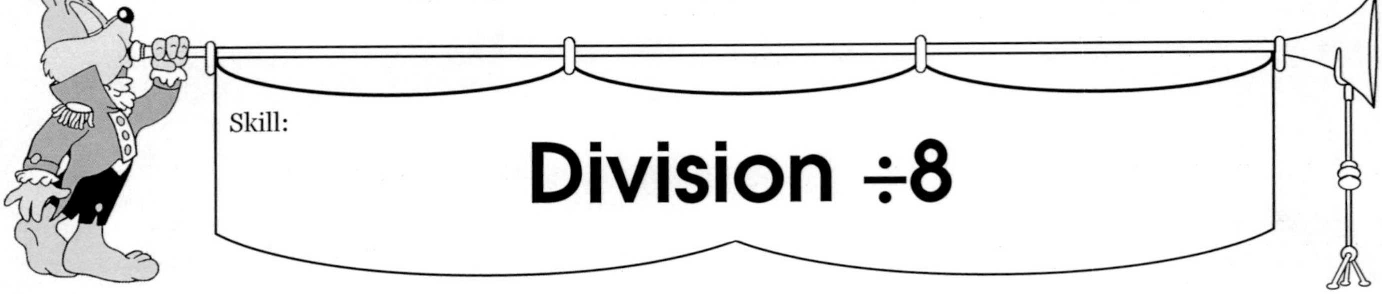

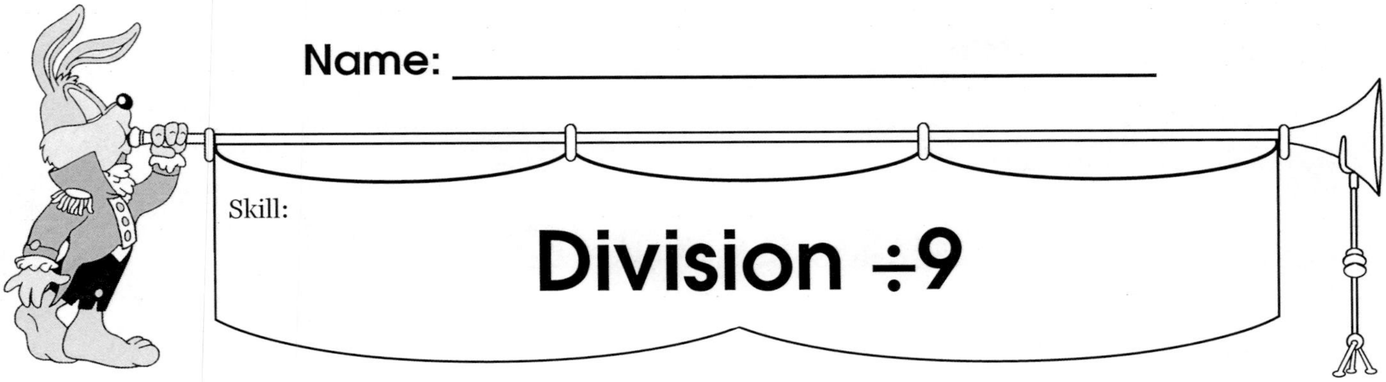

Skill:

Division ÷9

$$9)\overline{}^{3} \qquad 9)\overline{9} \qquad 9)\overline{45} \qquad 9)\overline{81} \qquad 9)\overline{}^{6}$$

$$9)\overline{18} \qquad 9)\overline{}^{8} \qquad 9)\overline{63} \qquad 9)\overline{36} \qquad 9)\overline{}^{10}$$

$9 + 9 + 9 + 9 + 9 =$ _____

_____ groups of the number _____   _____ $\div 9 = 5$

$18 \div 9 =$ _____ $90 \div 9 =$ _____

_____ $\div 9 = 4$ _____ $\div 9 = 7$

$72 \div 9 =$ _____   _____ $\div 9 = 1$

$54 \div 9 =$ _____ $81 \div 9 =$ _____

$27 \div 9 =$ _____   _____ $\div 9 = 5$

$9 + 9 + 9 + 9 + 9 + 9 + 9 =$ _____

_____ groups of the number _____ $63 \div 9 =$ _____

Number of Problems: 22   Number Correct: _____   Time to complete: _____ min.

Name: _____

Skill: _____

Division Review One

Divisors 1 to 9   **Without Remainders**

$5\overline{)15}$ $2\overline{)36}$ $6\overline{)}\,^{6}$ $8\overline{)64}$ $4\overline{)36}$

$7\overline{)21}$ $4\overline{)}\,^{8}$ $1\overline{)12}$ $9\overline{)}\,^{1}$ $6\overline{)42}$

$3\overline{)30}$ $6\overline{)48}$ $7\overline{)42}$ $5\overline{)}\,^{9}$ $2\overline{)18}$

$5\overline{)35}$ $8\overline{)}\,^{4}$ $2\overline{)60}$ $4\overline{)16}$ $9\overline{)18}$

$6\overline{)}\,^{8}$ $2\overline{)44}$ $5\overline{)50}$ $3\overline{)}\,^{9}$ $7\overline{)}\,^{2}$

$9\overline{)81}$ $7\overline{)}\,^{9}$ $1\overline{)6}$ $8\overline{)}\,^{5}$ $4\overline{)12}$

Number of Problems: 30   Number Correct: _____   Time to complete: ____ min.

Skill:

Division Review Two

Divisors 1 to 9   Without Remainders

$20 \div 5 = $ _____

$36 \div 4 = $ _____

$90 \div 9 = $ _____

_____ $\div 5 = 3$

_____ $\div 8 = 8$

$21 \div 3 = $ _____

$6 \div 1 = $ _____

_____ $\div 9 = 6$

$49 \div 7 = $ _____

_____ $\div 2 = 9$

_____ $\div 4 = 10$

$48 \div 8 = $ _____

_____ $\div 6 = 6$

_____ $\div 3 = 12$

_____ $\div 7 = 3$

$9 \div 3 = $ _____

$12 \div 2 = $ _____

$45 \div 5 = $ _____

_____ $\div 8 = 2$

$48 \div 4 = $ _____

$9 \div 1 = $ _____

_____ $\div 7 = 8$

$36 \div 2 = $ _____

$45 \div 9 = $ _____

_____ $\div 6 = 3$

$54 \div 6 = $ _____

$45 \div 3 = $ _____

$50 \div 5 = $ _____

$24 \div 2 = $ _____

$81 \div 9 = $ _____

Number of Problems: 30   Number Correct: _____   Time to complete: ____ min.

Name: _____

What's Missing?

Divisors 1 to 12   Without Remainders

a)
```
      1 1
  6 ) □ 6
      □
      0 6
        6
        0
```

b)
```
      1 □
  3 ) □ 6
      □
      0 6
        6
        0
```

c)
```
      1 4
  2 ) 2 □
      □
      0 □
        8
        0
```

d)
```
      0 8
  6 ) 4 □
      □ 8
        0
```

e)
```
      □ 3
  3 ) 9 9
      9
      □ 9
        □
        0
```

f)
```
      6 5
  1 ) □ □
```

g)
```
      1 0
  4 ) 4 0
      □
      0 0
        □
        0
```

h)
```
      1 □
  6 ) 7 8
      □
      1 □
      1 8
        □
```

i)
```
      □ 2
  5 ) 6 □
      5
      □ □
      1 0
        0
```

j)
```
      1 5
  3 ) 4 □
      3
      □ □
      1 5
        □
```

k)
```
       □ □
 12 ) 1 4 4
       □ 2
       □ 4
       2 □
         0
```

l)
```
       □ □
 10 ) 1 0 □
       1 0
       □ □
       0 0
         0
```

Number of Problems: 12   Number Correct: _____   Time to complete: ____ min.

Name: _____

Word Problems

2 and 3 Digit Numbers
By 1 and 2 Digit Divisors   **Without Remainders**

There are 14 tabby kittens at the animal shelter. If they make 2 equal groups, how many kittens will be in each group?

_____ kittens

Donna had 44 free fry coupons. She gave 2 coupons to each kid in her class. How many kids are in her class?

_____ kids

Lisa made 18 invitations to her birthday party. If she wants to separate them into 3 equal groups, how many invitations will there be in each group?

_____ invitations

At camp, Ryan hung up 78 towels. If each clothesline held 13 towels, how many clotheslines were needed?

_____ clotheslines

Sean caught 63 frogs in the ponds. He has separated them equally into 9 different kinds. How many frogs are there of each kind?

_____ frogs

At Pet World, there are 96 fish. Each aquarium holds 12 fish. How many aquariums are being used at the pet shop?

_____ aquariums

Dianne put 36 pictures in her scrapbook. If she put them into 3 equal groups, how many pictures will be in each group?

_____ pictures

In the library, there were 20 new computers installed. Each class got to use $\frac{1}{2}$ at a time. How many computers did each class use?

_____ computers

There are 144 marbles in the bucket. If you put them into 12 equal groups, how many marbles will there be in each group?

_____ marbles

In total, the 3 girls walked their dogs 12 blocks. If Veneda, Kelly, and Lisa walked equal distances, how far did they each walk their dogs?

_____ blocks

Number of Problems: 10   Number Correct: _____   Time to complete: ____ min.

Name: _____

One Digit Division

2 and 3 Digit Numbers By 1 Digit Divisors   **Without Remainders**

$9\overline{)108}$	$6\overline{)66}$	$2\overline{)48}$	$5\overline{)100}$	$8\overline{)872}$
$3\overline{)174}$	$9\overline{)819}$	$8\overline{)16}$	$4\overline{)52}$	$7\overline{)903}$
$5\overline{)85}$	$6\overline{)90}$	$9\overline{)468}$	$7\overline{)539}$	$4\overline{)324}$
$9\overline{)270}$	$2\overline{)90}$	$4\overline{)100}$	$6\overline{)408}$	$3\overline{)375}$
$7\overline{)994}$	$3\overline{)372}$	$6\overline{)696}$	$5\overline{)900}$	$2\overline{)144}$

Number of Problems: 25   Number Correct: _____   Time to complete: ____ min.

Name: _____

One Digit Division

**2 and 3 Digit Numbers
By 1 Digit Divisors**   **Without Remainders**

$72 \div 4 =$ _____ $198 \div 9 =$ _____ $60 \div 5 =$ _____

$966 \div 2 =$ _____ $10 \div 0 =$ _____ $550 \div 5 =$ _____

$48 \div 3 =$ _____ $616 \div 4 =$ _____ $516 \div 6 =$ _____

$128 \div 8 =$ _____ $81 \div 9 =$ _____ $294 \div 6 =$ _____

$504 \div 7 =$ _____ $95 \div 5 =$ _____ $822 \div 2 =$ _____

$228 \div 2 =$ _____ $436 \div 0 =$ _____ $45 \div 9 =$ _____

$240 \div 3 =$ _____ $92 \div 4 =$ _____ $390 \div 6 =$ _____

$88 \div 4 =$ _____ $352 \div 8 =$ _____ $49 \div 7 =$ _____

$111 \div 1 =$ _____ $850 \div 5 =$ _____ $720 \div 8 =$ _____

$22 \div 2 =$ _____ $342 \div 9 =$ _____ $99 \div 3 =$ _____

Number of Problems: 30   Number Correct: _____   Time to complete: _____ min.

Name: _____

One Digit Division

2 and 3 Digit Numbers By 1 Digit Divisors

With Remainders

9)82 4)54 7)11 2)67 8)93

8)881 7)750 3)95 9)95 5)649

4)89 2)365 6)491 8)100 5)486

3)998 9)26 5)428 6)227 4)37

7)44 8)671 5)24 2)93 9)991

Number of Problems: 25 Number Correct: _____ Time to complete: ____ min.

One Digit Division

2 and 3 Digit Numbers
By 1 Digit Divisors

With Remainders

$77 \div 3 =$ _____

$94 \div 9 =$ _____

$875 \div 9 =$ _____

$425 \div 2 =$ _____

$944 \div 3 =$ _____

$605 \div 4 =$ _____

$77 \div 2 =$ _____

$911 \div 2 =$ _____

$707 \div 3 =$ _____

$111 \div 7 =$ _____

$364 \div 5 =$ _____

$503 \div 7 =$ _____

$89 \div 7 =$ _____

$13 \div 5 =$ _____

$928 \div 7 =$ _____

$32 \div 9 =$ _____

$384 \div 5 =$ _____

$47 \div 4 =$ _____

$832 \div 9 =$ _____

$423 \div 5 =$ _____

$607 \div 8 =$ _____

$793 \div 6 =$ _____

$213 \div 4 =$ _____

$321 \div 8 =$ _____

$71 \div 6 =$ _____

$869 \div 6 =$ _____

$99 \div 7 =$ _____

$524 \div 8 =$ _____

$16 \div 3 =$ _____

$54 \div 4 =$ _____

Number of Problems: 30   Number Correct: _____   Time to complete: ____ min.

Skill:

One Digit Division

3 and 4 Digit Numbers By 1 Digit Divisors

Without Remainders

$4\overline{)444}$ $8\overline{)448}$ $2\overline{)822}$ $5\overline{)925}$ $7\overline{)210}$

$9\overline{)9054}$ $5\overline{)665}$ $3\overline{)471}$ $6\overline{)222}$ $4\overline{)5092}$

$2\overline{)802}$ $6\overline{)5556}$ $4\overline{)196}$ $7\overline{)4123}$ $8\overline{)592}$

$7\overline{)2023}$ $9\overline{)2511}$ $3\overline{)318}$ $5\overline{)9480}$ $6\overline{)7356}$

Number of Problems: 20   Number Correct: _____   Time to complete: ____ min.

One Digit Division

Skill:

3 and 4 Digit Numbers By 1 Digit Divisors

Without Remainders

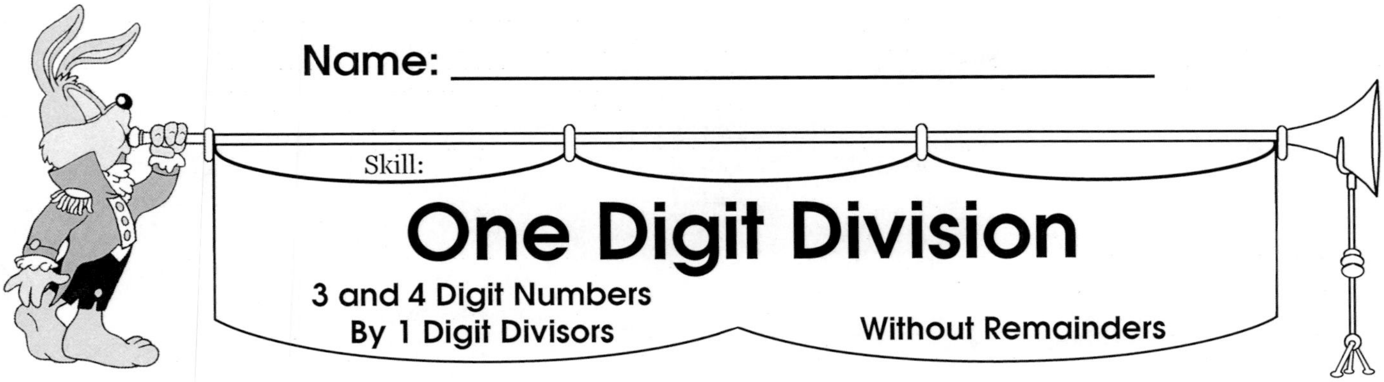

$8496 \div 2 =$ _____ $9618 \div 7 =$ _____ $324 \div 4 =$ _____

$450 \div 9 =$ _____ $6480 \div 3 =$ _____ $732 \div 4 =$ _____

$4500 \div 9 =$ _____ $665 \div 5 =$ _____ $7408 \div 8 =$ _____

$948 \div 6 =$ _____ $3374 \div 7 =$ _____ $888 \div 2 =$ _____

$1158 \div 6 =$ _____ $384 \div 3 =$ _____ $9936 \div 9 =$ _____

$453 \div 3 =$ _____ $2005 \div 5 =$ _____ $5064 \div 4 =$ _____

$8211 \div 7 =$ _____ $168 \div 8 =$ _____ $6354 \div 9 =$ _____

$4627 \div 7 =$ _____ $588 \div 6 =$ _____ $7195 \div 5 =$ _____

$1212 \div 6 =$ _____ $8355 \div 5 =$ _____ $3928 \div 8 =$ _____

$6720 \div 4 =$ _____ $4347 \div 9 =$ _____ $2457 \div 3 =$ _____

Number of Problems: 30   Number Correct: _____   Time to complete: ____ min.

Name: _____

Skill:

One Digit Division

3 and 4 Digit Numbers
By 1 Digit Divisors   With Remainders

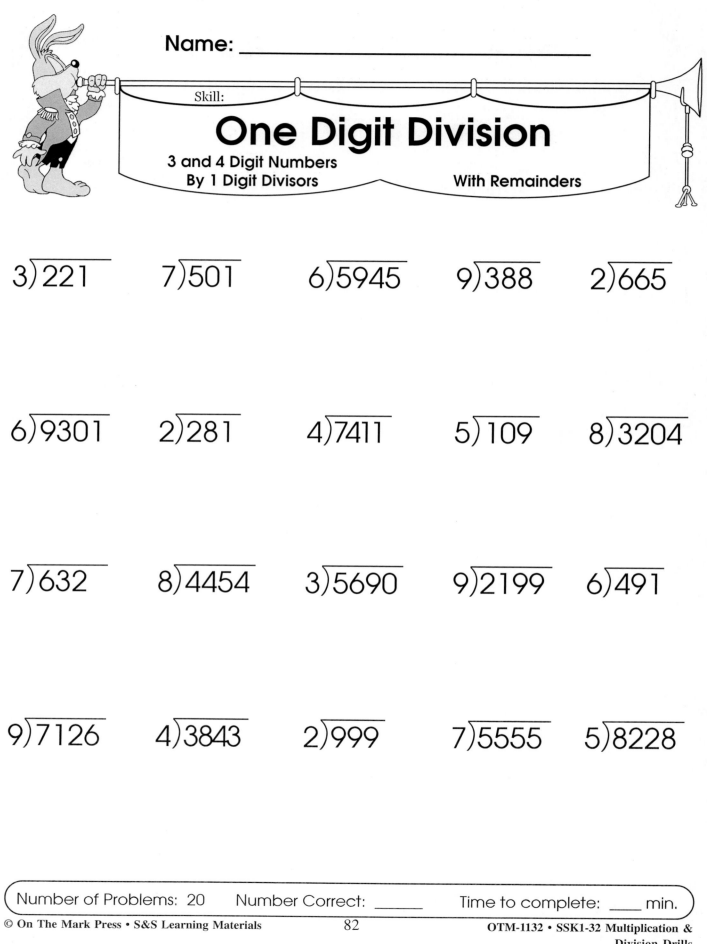

$3\overline{)221}$ $7\overline{)501}$ $6\overline{)5945}$ $9\overline{)388}$ $2\overline{)665}$

$6\overline{)9301}$ $2\overline{)281}$ $4\overline{)7411}$ $5\overline{)109}$ $8\overline{)3204}$

$7\overline{)632}$ $8\overline{)4454}$ $3\overline{)5690}$ $9\overline{)2199}$ $6\overline{)491}$

$9\overline{)7126}$ $4\overline{)3843}$ $2\overline{)999}$ $7\overline{)5555}$ $5\overline{)8228}$

Number of Problems: 20   Number Correct: _____   Time to complete: ____ min.

Skill:

One Digit Division

3 and 4 Digit Numbers
By 1 Digit Divisors

With Remainders

671 ÷ 5 = _____

5941 ÷ 2 = _____

427 ÷ 9 = _____

7334 ÷ 4 = _____

914 ÷ 7 = _____

4354 ÷ 9 = _____

203 ÷ 4 = _____

3844 ÷ 6 = _____

101 ÷ 3 = _____

6348 ÷ 8 = _____

811 ÷ 2 = _____

1843 ÷ 7 = _____

2991 ÷ 8 = _____

5959 ÷ 5 = _____

344 ÷ 9 = _____

6116 ÷ 6 = _____

5113 ÷ 8 = _____

724 ÷ 3 = _____

4943 ÷ 7 = _____

9655 ÷ 2 = _____

229 ÷ 4 = _____

1194 ÷ 5 = _____

8144 ÷ 9 = _____

7989 ÷ 8 = _____

2637 ÷ 7 = _____

3963 ÷ 7 = _____

2111 ÷ 2 = _____

945 ÷ 6 = _____

6992 ÷ 3 = _____

5182 ÷ 4 = _____

Number of Problems: 30   Number Correct: _____   Time to complete: ____ min.

Skill:

One Digit Division

**4 and 5 Digit Numbers
By 1 Digit Divisors**   **Without Remainders**

$3\overline{)3654}$ $9\overline{)8181}$ $4\overline{)2492}$ $7\overline{)6496}$ $5\overline{)5555}$

$6\overline{)1548}$ $7\overline{)45388}$ $8\overline{)7328}$ $2\overline{)39826}$ $9\overline{)8766}$

$9\overline{)87660}$ $8\overline{)2848}$ $3\overline{)62469}$ $4\overline{)5784}$ $7\overline{)14868}$

$4\overline{)41324}$ $2\overline{)76460}$ $9\overline{)3258}$ $6\overline{)83550}$ $3\overline{)22221}$

Number of Problems: 20   Number Correct: _____   Time to complete: ____ min.

One Digit Division

Skill:

**4 and 5 Digit Numbers
By 1 Digit Divisors**

Without Remainders

6309 ÷ 9 = _____   92142 ÷ 3 = _____   4452 ÷ 6 = _____

81232 ÷ 8 = _____   2110 ÷ 2 = _____   1232 ÷ 8 = _____

77886 ÷ 6 = _____   31224 ÷ 4 = _____   5901 ÷ 7 = _____

67555 ÷ 5 = _____   96231 ÷ 3 = _____   41678 ÷ 2 = _____

3632 ÷ 8 = _____   24684 ÷ 6 = _____   7596 ÷ 9 = _____

71536 ÷ 4 = _____   62109 ÷ 9 = _____   8883 ÷ 7 = _____

53157 ÷ 3 = _____   98985 ÷ 5 = _____   38294 ÷ 2 = _____

15448 ÷ 8 = _____   48474 ÷ 9 = _____   9996 ÷ 4 = _____

27559 ÷ 7 = _____   71106 ÷ 7 = _____   83448 ÷ 6 = _____

6879 ÷ 3 = _____   59422 ÷ 2 = _____   31695 ÷ 5 = _____

Number of Problems: 30   Number Correct: _____   Time to complete: ____ min.

Skill:

One Digit Division

**4 and 5 Digit Numbers
By 1 Digit Divisors**   **With Remainders**

$6 \overline{)2157}$ $\quad$ $2 \overline{)75421}$ $\quad$ $5 \overline{)42366}$ $\quad$ $9 \overline{)6951}$ $\quad$ $3 \overline{)94325}$

$9 \overline{)56123}$ $\quad$ $5 \overline{)7177}$ $\quad$ $7 \overline{)36542}$ $\quad$ $8 \overline{)26348}$ $\quad$ $4 \overline{)8321}$

$3 \overline{)49769}$ $\quad$ $4 \overline{)3455}$ $\quad$ $9 \overline{)5248}$ $\quad$ $4 \overline{)61141}$ $\quad$ $7 \overline{)72727}$

$7 \overline{)9999}$ $\quad$ $2 \overline{)87659}$ $\quad$ $6 \overline{)4115}$ $\quad$ $3 \overline{)23197}$ $\quad$ $8 \overline{)94327}$

Number of Problems: 20 $\quad$ Number Correct: _____ $\quad$ Time to complete: ____ min.

One Digit Division

**4 and 5 Digit Numbers
By 1 Digit Divisors**   **With Remainders**

$2154 \div 7 =$ _____ $51239 \div 4 =$ _____ $6758 \div 9 =$ _____

$36899 \div 3 =$ _____ $8369 \div 6 =$ _____ $74771 \div 2 =$ _____

$1333 \div 3 =$ _____ $97748 \div 5 =$ _____ $4500 \div 7 =$ _____

$55455 \div 4 =$ _____ $9229 \div 9 =$ _____ $34178 \div 8 =$ _____

$7450 \div 6 =$ _____ $87447 \div 2 =$ _____ $77238 \div 5 =$ _____

$18571 \div 4 =$ _____ $3777 \div 7 =$ _____ $41327 \div 3 =$ _____

$6235 \div 8 =$ _____ $26751 \div 9 =$ _____ $59942 \div 6 =$ _____

$71344 \div 5 =$ _____ $1515 \div 4 =$ _____ $93457 \div 2 =$ _____

$4733 \div 3 =$ _____ $88288 \div 3 =$ _____ $64934 \div 9 =$ _____

$9779 \div 8 =$ _____ $22925 \div 6 =$ _____ $35577 \div 7 =$ _____

Number of Problems: 30   Number Correct: _____   Time to complete: ____ min.

Skill:

Division Review Three

2 to 5 Digit Numbers
By 1 Digit Divisors

Without Remainders

$8\overline{)88}$ $4\overline{)540}$ $7\overline{)7161}$ $2\overline{)45620}$ $5\overline{)355}$

$6\overline{)2694}$ $2\overline{)6744}$ $9\overline{)19197}$ $3\overline{)843}$ $7\overline{)76496}$

$5\overline{)445}$ $3\overline{)16431}$ $8\overline{)5128}$ $4\overline{)92}$ $6\overline{)3966}$

$9\overline{)837}$ $4\overline{)4348}$ $6\overline{)54324}$ $5\overline{)1115}$ $2\overline{)622}$

Number of Problems: 20   Number Correct: _____   Time to complete: ____ min.

Skill:

Division Review Four

2 to 5 Digit Numbers
By 1 Digit Divisors   Without Remainders

$711 \div 3 =$ _____

$77777 \div 7 =$ _____

$3636 \div 9 =$ _____

$95 \div 5 =$ _____

$2604 \div 6 =$ _____

$54306 \div 9 =$ _____

$650 \div 5 =$ _____

$41484 \div 6 =$ _____

$9320 \div 8 =$ _____

$49 \div 7 =$ _____

$8136 \div 6 =$ _____

$26992 \div 8 =$ _____

$304 \div 4 =$ _____

$79122 \div 3 =$ _____

$588 \div 2 =$ _____

$69433 \div 7 =$ _____

$438 \div 2 =$ _____

$5211 \div 9 =$ _____

$64 \div 4 =$ _____

$51630 \div 5 =$ _____

$72 \div 8 =$ _____

$1635 \div 3 =$ _____

$84924 \div 6 =$ _____

$364 \div 4 =$ _____

$4748 \div 2 =$ _____

$3095 \div 5 =$ _____

$25470 \div 9 =$ _____

$35 \div 7 =$ _____

$6176 \div 8 =$ _____

$31314 \div 3 =$ _____

Number of Problems: 30   Number Correct: _____   Time to complete: ____ min.

Name: _____

Division Review Five

**2 to 5 Digit Numbers
By 1 Digit Divisors**   **With Remainders**

$9\overline{)65406}$ $2\overline{)109}$ $6\overline{)3458}$ $8\overline{)275}$ $4\overline{)91}$

$5\overline{)5248}$ $8\overline{)28503}$ $7\overline{)61}$ $3\overline{)4397}$ $9\overline{)81537}$

$6\overline{)707}$ $4\overline{)9041}$ $3\overline{)39148}$ $2\overline{)1111}$ $5\overline{)6721}$

$8\overline{)29359}$ $7\overline{)853}$ $9\overline{)4107}$ $4\overline{)33}$ $6\overline{)76546}$

Number of Problems: 20   Number Correct: _____   Time to complete: ____ min.

Skill: _____

Division Review Six

2 to 5 Digit Numbers
By 1 Digit Divisors   **With Remainders**

$411 \div 5 =$ _____ $9692 \div 3 =$ _____ $273 \div 9 =$ _____

$799 \div 2 =$ _____ $50544 \div 7 =$ _____ $11 \div 6 =$ _____

$36620 \div 9 =$ _____ $815 \div 4 =$ _____ $4931 \div 8 =$ _____

$2153 \div 3 =$ _____ $7321 \div 2 =$ _____ $65 \div 7 =$ _____

$11498 \div 6 =$ _____ $86301 \div 5 =$ _____ $322 \div 4 =$ _____

$50329 \div 9 =$ _____ $4865 \div 3 =$ _____ $701 \div 8 =$ _____

$2161 \div 2 =$ _____ $93218 \div 7 =$ _____ $355 \div 8 =$ _____

$67904 \div 5 =$ _____ $8163 \div 4 =$ _____ $74318 \div 9 =$ _____

$51 \div 6 =$ _____ $5599 \div 3 =$ _____ $20209 \div 2 =$ _____

$468 \div 7 =$ _____ $99984 \div 5 =$ _____ $31499 \div 4 =$ _____

Number of Problems: 30   Number Correct: _____   Time to complete: ____ min.

Name: _____

What's Missing?

2 to 5 Digit Numbers
By 1 Digit Divisors
Without Remainders

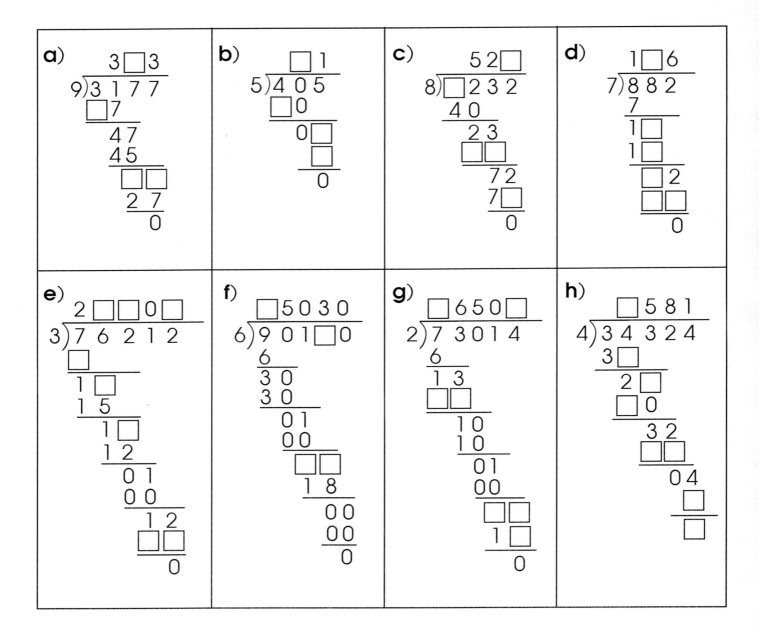

a)

```
    3 □ 3
9 ) 3 1 7 7
    □ 7
    4 7
    4 5
    □ □
    2 7
    0
```

b)

```
      □ 1
5 ) 4 0 5
    □ 0
    0 □
      □
      0
```

c)

```
      5 2 □
8 ) □ 2 3 2
    4 0
    2 3
    □ □
    7 2
    7 □
    0
```

d)

```
      1 □ 6
7 ) 8 8 2
    7
    1 □
    1 □
    □ 2
    □ □
    0
```

e)

```
    2 □ □ 0 □
3 ) 7 6 2 1 2
    □
    1 □
    1 5
    1 □
    1 2
    0 1
    0 0
    1 2
    □ □
    0
```

f)

```
    □ 5 0 3 0
6 ) 9 0 1 □ 0
    6
    3 0
    3 0
    0 1
    0 0
    □ □
    1 8
    0 0
    0 0
    0
```

g)

```
    □ 6 5 0 □
2 ) 7 3 0 1 4
    6
    1 3
    □ □
    1 0
    1 0
    0 1
    0 0
    □ □
    1 □
    0
```

h)

```
    □ 5 8 1
4 ) 3 4 3 2 4
    3 □
    2 □
    □ 0
    3 2
    □ □
    0 4
    □
    □
```

Number of Problems: 8   Number Correct: _____   Time to complete: ____ min.

© On The Mark Press • S&S Learning Materials   92   OTM-1132 • SSK1-32 Multiplication & Division Drills

Name: _____

What's Missing?

**2 to 5 Digit Numbers
By 1 Digit Divisors**

With Remainders

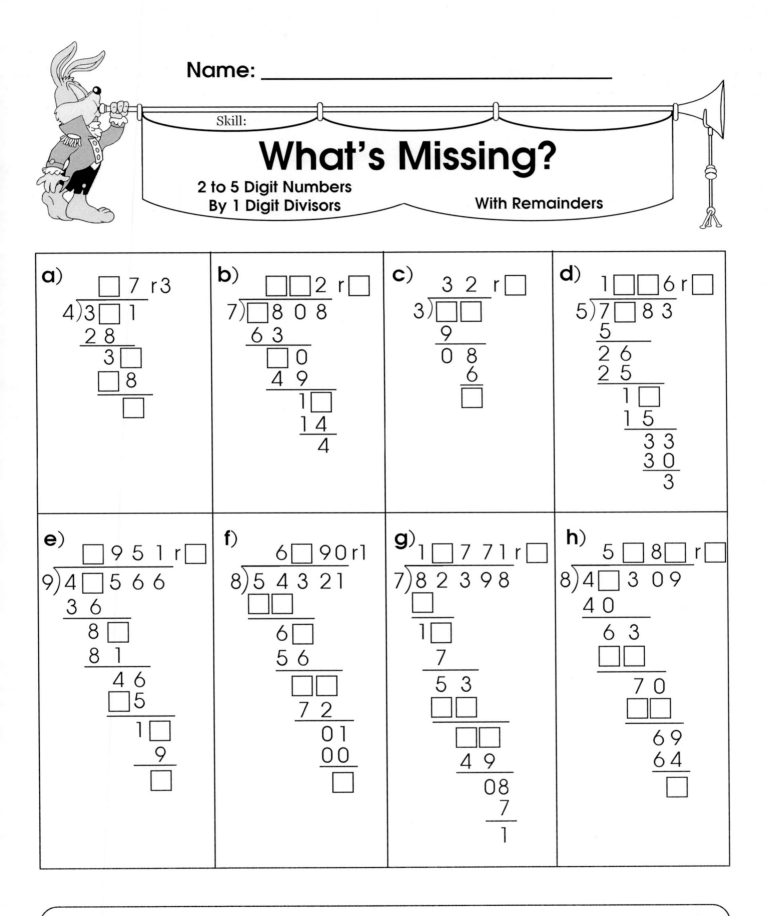

a)	b)	c)	d)
e)	f)	g)	h)

Number of Problems: 8   Number Correct: _____   Time to complete: ____ min.

Skill:

Word Problems

3 to 5 Digit Numbers
By 1 Digit Divisors

Mr. Walsh's class went on an overnight hiking trip to Mount Washington. The students hiked 14 504 meters in 6 hours on the first day and 13, 381 meters in 5 hours on the second day. How many meters walked did the students average per hour over the two day hike?

A wealthy landowner decided to donate 125 acres of land each to his 6 favorite charities. His total land ownership was 1 062 acres. How much did the landowner have left after his donation?

Kira's race swim times were 481, 498, 489, 477, 478, 497, 497, 483, and 490 seconds. In order for Kira to advance to the National swim meet, she would have to average 484 seconds in her best 6 races. Did she qualify for the Nationals?

Kyle works on the line in a packaging factory inspecting and wrapping up chocolates. Today his goal is to process 15 520 chocolates in his 8-hour shift. If he can reach his goal, he is allowed to take home a free box of chocolates. On average, how many chocolates per hour does Kyle have to process in order to get the free chocolates?

Janet does all the photocopying for H.H. Langford School. Last week between Monday and Friday, she copied 18 540 copies for all 9 classrooms. On average, how many copies did Janet make for each class each day?

Number of Problems: 5   Number Correct: _____   Time to complete: ____ min.

Skill: _____

Divisibility Table

2 and 3 Digit Numbers
By 1 Digit Divisors   Without Remainders

Circle **yes** if the number is divisable by the given number. Circle **no** if the number is not divisible by the given number.

64 by			112 by			600 by			90 by		
4	yes	no	2	yes	no	2	yes	no	2	yes	no
5	yes	no	3	yes	no	3	yes	no	4	yes	no
6	yes	no	5	yes	no	5	yes	no	5	yes	no
7	yes	no	7	yes	no	6	yes	no	6	yes	no
8	yes	no	9	yes	no	7	yes	no	9	yes	no

228 by			552 by			696 by			808 by		
2	yes	no	2	yes	no	2	yes	no	2	yes	no
4	yes	no	3	yes	no	4	yes	no	3	yes	no
5	yes	no	4	yes	no	6	yes	no	4	yes	no
7	yes	no	6	yes	no	7	yes	no	6	yes	no
8	yes	no	9	yes	no	8	yes	no	7	yes	no

Number of Problems: 40   Number Correct: _____   Time to complete: ____ min.

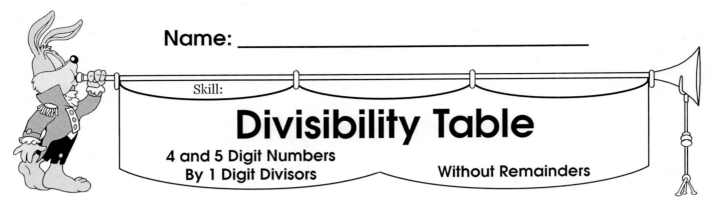

Name: _____

Skill: _____

Divisibility Table

**4 and 5 Digit Numbers
By 1 Digit Divisors**   **Without Remainders**

Circle **yes** if the number is divisable by the given number. Circle **no** if the number is not divisible by the given number.

1 747
by

2	yes	no
5	yes	no
6	yes	no
7	yes	no
8	yes	no

98 400
by

2	yes	no
3	yes	no
4	yes	no
5	yes	no
6	yes	no

15 051
by

3	yes	no
5	yes	no
7	yes	no
8	yes	no
9	yes	no

2 355
by

4	yes	no
5	yes	no
6	yes	no
7	yes	no
8	yes	no

11 606
by

2	yes	no
3	yes	no
6	yes	no
7	yes	no
9	yes	no

5 428
by

4	yes	no
6	yes	no
7	yes	no
8	yes	no
9	yes	no

8 989
by

2	yes	no
3	yes	no
4	yes	no
6	yes	no
8	yes	no

67 401
by

3	yes	no
4	yes	no
5	yes	no
6	yes	no
7	yes	no

Number of Problems: 40   Number Correct: _____   Time to complete: ____ min.

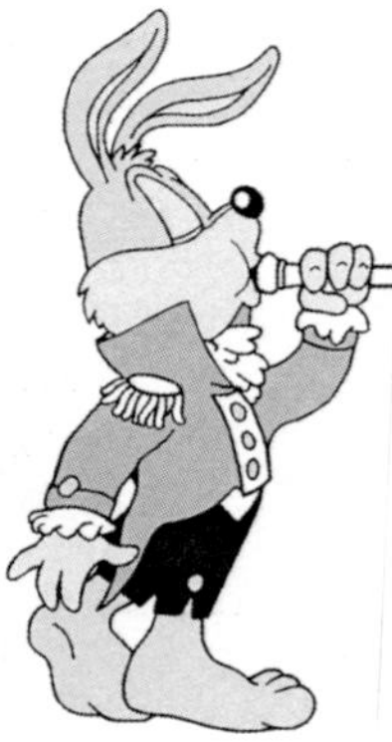

Name: ____________________________________

Skill:

Two Digit Division

2 Digit Numbers
By 2 Digit Divisors

Without Remainders

$20\overline{)80}$	$13\overline{)65}$	$11\overline{)99}$	$33\overline{)99}$
$15\overline{)60}$	$45\overline{)90}$	$14\overline{)98}$	$27\overline{)81}$
$16\overline{)64}$	$32\overline{)64}$	$13\overline{)91}$	$19\overline{)95}$
$12\overline{)24}$	$25\overline{)75}$	$22\overline{)88}$	$44\overline{)88}$
$28\overline{)84}$	$32\overline{)96}$	$17\overline{)85}$	$48\overline{)96}$

Number of Problems: 20 Number Correct: ______ Time to complete: ____ min.

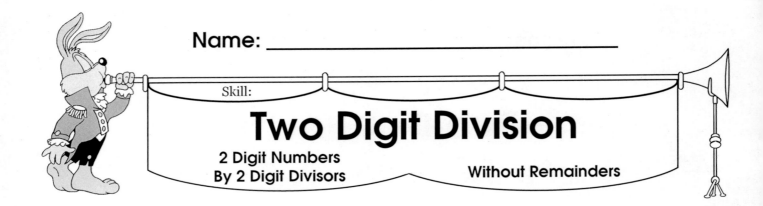

Name: _____

Two Digit Division

2 Digit Numbers
By 2 Digit Divisors

Without Remainders

$92 \div 46 =$ _____ $62 \div 31 =$ _____ $70 \div 14 =$ _____

$78 \div 26 =$ _____ $68 \div 34 =$ _____ $76 \div 19 =$ _____

$66 \div 22 =$ _____ $43 \div 43 =$ _____ $52 \div 13 =$ _____

$84 \div 42 =$ _____ $90 \div 30 =$ _____ $70 \div 35 =$ _____

$84 \div 28 =$ _____ $77 \div 11 =$ _____ $60 \div 20 =$ _____

$88 \div 44 =$ _____ $82 \div 41 =$ _____ $18 \div 18 =$ _____

$58 \div 29 =$ _____ $72 \div 12 =$ _____ $90 \div 15 =$ _____

$94 \div 47 =$ _____ $84 \div 21 =$ _____ $96 \div 32 =$ _____

Number of Problems: 24   Number Correct: _____   Time to complete: ____ min.

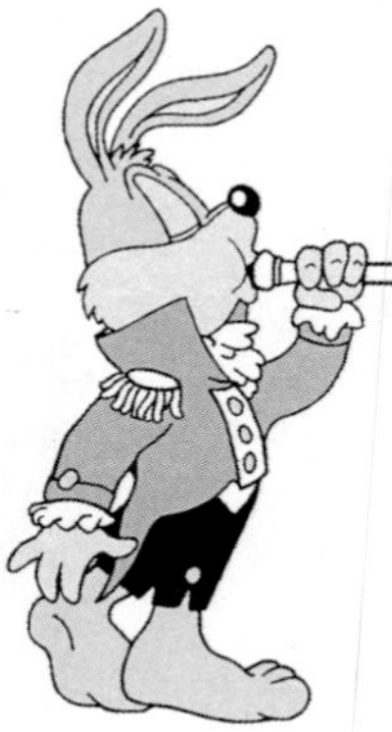

Name: _____

Two Digit Division

**2 Digit Numbers
By 2 Digit Divisors**
With Remainders

$18\overline{)75}$ $31\overline{)99}$ $12\overline{)40}$ $24\overline{)97}$

$21\overline{)66}$ $11\overline{)81}$ $33\overline{)34}$ $47\overline{)51}$

$35\overline{)79}$ $50\overline{)55}$ $16\overline{)31}$ $20\overline{)82}$

$19\overline{)91}$ $14\overline{)74}$ $28\overline{)80}$ $67\overline{)76}$

$91\overline{)92}$ $44\overline{)65}$ $39\overline{)93}$ $26\overline{)89}$

Number of Problems: 20   Number Correct: _____   Time to complete: ____ min.

Skill: _____

Two Digit Division

**2 Digit Numbers
By 2 Digit Divisors**   **With Remainders**

99 ÷ 17 = _____   54 ÷ 30 = _____   80 ÷ 67 = _____

91 ÷ 29 = _____   89 ÷ 44 = _____   48 ÷ 21 = _____

96 ÷ 90 = _____   81 ÷ 35 = _____   91 ÷ 81 = _____

13 ÷ 12 = _____   58 ÷ 39 = _____   55 ÷ 16 = _____

74 ÷ 32 = _____   94 ÷ 19 = _____   66 ÷ 24 = _____

58 ÷ 48 = _____   78 ÷ 70 = _____   86 ÷ 15 = _____

85 ÷ 41 = _____   84 ÷ 31 = _____   83 ÷ 26 = _____

51 ÷ 38 = _____   78 ÷ 11 = _____   90 ÷ 54 = _____

Number of Problems: 24   Number Correct: _____   Time to complete: ____ min.

Name: _____

Two Digit Division

**2 and 3 Digit Numbers
By 2 Digit Divisors**

Without Remainders

$26\overline{)468}$ $\qquad$ $43\overline{)86}$ $\qquad$ $92\overline{)736}$ $\qquad$ $31\overline{)93}$

$19\overline{)114}$ $\qquad$ $66\overline{)66}$ $\qquad$ $22\overline{)924}$ $\qquad$ $79\overline{)553}$

$41\overline{)82}$ $\qquad$ $11\overline{)748}$ $\qquad$ $35\overline{)70}$ $\qquad$ $58\overline{)870}$

$38\overline{)380}$ $\qquad$ $72\overline{)432}$ $\qquad$ $18\overline{)90}$ $\qquad$ $47\overline{)799}$

$16\overline{)64}$ $\qquad$ $25\overline{)950}$ $\qquad$ $55\overline{)55}$ $\qquad$ $80\overline{)400}$

Number of Problems: 20   Number Correct: _____   Time to complete: ____ min.

Name: _____

Two Digit Division

**2 and 3 Digit Numbers
By 2 Digit Divisors** **Without Remainders**

$426 \div 71 =$ _____ $84 \div 21 =$ _____ $768 \div 48 =$ _____

$102 \div 34 =$ _____ $65 \div 13 =$ _____ $936 \div 39 =$ _____

$100 \div 50 =$ _____ $801 \div 89 =$ _____ $840 \div 42 =$ _____

$144 \div 12 =$ _____ $77 \div 77 =$ _____ $598 \div 26 =$ _____

$924 \div 84 =$ _____ $99 \div 33 =$ _____ $80 \div 16 =$ _____

$272 \div 68 =$ _____ $42 \div 14 =$ _____ $609 \div 29 =$ _____

$703 \div 37 =$ _____ $86 \div 43 =$ _____ $726 \div 33 =$ _____

$133 \div 19 =$ _____ $316 \div 79 =$ _____ $484 \div 22 =$ _____

Number of Problems: 24   Number Correct: _____   Time to complete: ____ min.

Name: _____

Two Digit Division

**2 and 3 Digit Numbers
By 2 Digit Divisors**   **With Remainders**

$17\overline{)491}$　　　　$66\overline{)72}$　　　　$20\overline{)785}$　　　　$41\overline{)320}$

$36\overline{)689}$　　　　$78\overline{)87}$　　　　$92\overline{)919}$　　　　$18\overline{)99}$

$24\overline{)764}$　　　　$56\overline{)501}$　　　　$44\overline{)89}$　　　　$13\overline{)293}$

$88\overline{)188}$　　　　$11\overline{)61}$　　　　$32\overline{)903}$　　　　$61\overline{)111}$

$48\overline{)863}$　　　　$18\overline{)368}$　　　　$82\overline{)444}$　　　　$29\overline{)698}$

Number of Problems: 20   Number Correct: _____   Time to complete: ____ min.

Name: _____

Two Digit Division

2 and 3 Digit Numbers
By 2 Digit Divisors   **With Remainders**

$933 \div 61 =$ _____ $126 \div 27 =$ _____ $404 \div 19 =$ _____

$631 \div 31 =$ _____ $78 \div 51 =$ _____ $554 \div 15 =$ _____

$760 \div 44 =$ _____ $333 \div 72 =$ _____ $804 \div 33 =$ _____

$188 \div 81 =$ _____ $99 \div 96 =$ _____ $224 \div 24 =$ _____

$674 \div 18 =$ _____ $76 \div 26 =$ _____ $346 \div 56 =$ _____

$566 \div 68 =$ _____ $228 \div 48 =$ _____ $409 \div 88 =$ _____

$753 \div 36 =$ _____ $44 \div 17 =$ _____ $106 \div 60 =$ _____

$39 \div 16 =$ _____ $899 \div 25 =$ _____ $501 \div 11 =$ _____

| Number of Problems: 24 | Number Correct: _____ | Time to complete: ____ min. |

Name: _____

Two Digit Division

**3 and 4 Digit Numbers
By 2 Digit Divisors**   **Without Remainders**

73)584   21)2100   15)4545   34)442

40)2160   11)616   54)4644   96)576

63)189   16)3168   24)408   44)8712

28)2520   52)988   82)7626   17)884

19)912   27)5049   42)6552   67)8308

Number of Problems: 20   Number Correct: _____   Time to complete: _____ min.

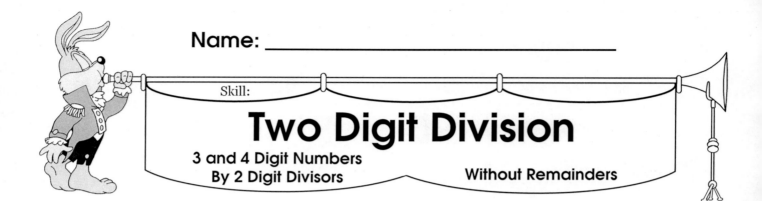

Skill: _____

Two Digit Division

**3 and 4 Digit Numbers
By 2 Digit Divisors**

Without Remainders

1034 ÷ 47 = _____   288 ÷ 12 = _____   2160 ÷ 36 = _____

567 ÷ 63 = _____   6250 ÷ 50 = _____   330 ÷ 66 = _____

7029 ÷ 99 = _____   437 ÷ 23 = _____   858 ÷ 11 = _____

6808 ÷ 74 = _____   943 ÷ 41 = _____   3937 ÷ 31 = _____

5896 ÷ 22 = _____   234 ÷ 39 = _____   169 ÷ 13 = _____

1320 ÷ 55 = _____   4958 ÷ 67 = _____   3870 ÷ 43 = _____

832 ÷ 26 = _____   5568 ÷ 96 = _____   1196 ÷ 92 = _____

825 ÷ 15 = _____   6936 ÷ 51 = _____   2376 ÷ 44 = _____

Number of Problems: 24   Number Correct: _____   Time to complete: ____ min.

Skill: _____

Two Digit Division

3 and 4 Digit Numbers
By 2 Digit Divisors

With Remainders

$80\overline{)807}$ $\qquad$ $33\overline{)663}$ $\qquad$ $67\overline{)6556}$ $\qquad$ $20\overline{)3788}$

$58\overline{)5391}$ $\qquad$ $24\overline{)1359}$ $\qquad$ $47\overline{)576}$ $\qquad$ $14\overline{)923}$

$12\overline{)9355}$ $\qquad$ $77\overline{)1952}$ $\qquad$ $82\overline{)404}$ $\qquad$ $55\overline{)500}$

$62\overline{)1161}$ $\qquad$ $44\overline{)3806}$ $\qquad$ $71\overline{)5614}$ $\qquad$ $38\overline{)252}$

$23\overline{)763}$ $\qquad$ $16\overline{)7320}$ $\qquad$ $54\overline{)544}$ $\qquad$ $41\overline{)8141}$

Number of Problems: 20	Number Correct: _____	Time to complete: ____ min.

Name: _____

Two Digit Division

3 and 4 Digit Numbers
By 2 Digit Divisors

With Remainders

$7544 \div 63 =$ _____ $208 \div 22 =$ _____ $3654 \div 99 =$ _____

$777 \div 48 =$ _____ $4580 \div 76 =$ _____ $632 \div 43 =$ _____

$519 \div 35 =$ _____ $2352 \div 52 =$ _____ $404 \div 24 =$ _____

$8222 \div 83 =$ _____ $677 \div 67 =$ _____ $9671 \div 92 =$ _____

$5723 \div 32 =$ _____ $545 \div 45 =$ _____ $339 \div 28 =$ _____

$1331 \div 72 =$ _____ $207 \div 57 =$ _____ $4752 \div 65 =$ _____

$1994 \div 89 =$ _____ $6416 \div 41 =$ _____ $8281 \div 97 =$ _____

$999 \div 25 =$ _____ $8975 \div 75 =$ _____ $7094 \div 69 =$ _____

Number of Problems: 24   Number Correct: _____   Time to complete: ____ min.

Name: _____

Two Digit Division

**4 and 5 Digit Numbers
By 2 Digit Divisors**   **Without Remainders**

$37\overline{)5772}$ $76\overline{)76076}$ $48\overline{)2304}$ $13\overline{)71500}$

$55\overline{)15180}$ $67\overline{)4489}$ $91\overline{)39494}$ $87\overline{)2001}$

$27\overline{)4455}$ $42\overline{)80976}$ $24\overline{)6792}$ $19\overline{)72998}$

$18\overline{)37494}$ $81\overline{)4374}$ $53\overline{)9169}$ $32\overline{)52992}$

$62\overline{)6448}$ $97\overline{)28906}$ $79\overline{)85004}$ $21\overline{)7182}$

Number of Problems: 20   Number Correct: _____   Time to complete: ____ min.

Skill:

Two Digit Division

**4 and 5 Digit Numbers
By 2 Digit Divisors**   **Without Remainders**

$2580 \div 43 =$ _____ $11780 \div 76 =$ _____ $4563 \div 27 =$ _____

$66436 \div 68 =$ _____ $98800 \div 19 =$ _____ $7560 \div 63 =$ _____

$33511 \div 31 =$ _____ $5175 \div 45 =$ _____ $6192 \div 72 =$ _____

$48884 \div 22 =$ _____ $8484 \div 42 =$ _____ $24157 \div 17 =$ _____

$53988 \div 33 =$ _____ $43940 \div 65 =$ _____ $9282 \div 42 =$ _____

$18975 \div 55 =$ _____ $8160 \div 24 =$ _____ $33000 \div 75 =$ _____

$75990 \div 15 =$ _____ $23959 \div 97 =$ _____ $38976 \div 48 =$ _____

$54984 \div 87 =$ _____ $6960 \div 29 =$ _____ $40950 \div 70 =$ _____

Number of Problems: 24   Number Correct: _____   Time to complete: ____ min.

Skill:

Two Digit Division

4 and 5 Digit Numbers
By 2 Digit Divisors

With Remainders

$54 \overline{)6722}$ $16 \overline{)16513}$ $38 \overline{)2792}$ $81 \overline{)96440}$

$26 \overline{)38951}$ $78 \overline{)7070}$ $94 \overline{)45607}$ $67 \overline{)8180}$

$18 \overline{)1309}$ $63 \overline{)53620}$ $44 \overline{)6544}$ $33 \overline{)23143}$

$92 \overline{)90817}$ $24 \overline{)3424}$ $73 \overline{)85398}$ $57 \overline{)7767}$

$83 \overline{)2100}$ $32 \overline{)46502}$ $66 \overline{)2929}$ $15 \overline{)14494}$

Number of Problems: 20   Number Correct: _____   Time to complete: ____ min.

Name: _____

Two Digit Division

**4 and 5 Digit Numbers
By 2 Digit Divisors**

With Remainders

$4434 \div 43 =$ _____

$19823 \div 68 =$ _____

$7368 \div 18 =$ _____

$30927 \div 76 =$ _____

$76543 \div 11 =$ _____

$2786 \div 38 =$ _____

$52159 \div 92 =$ _____

$6446 \div 44 =$ _____

$8103 \div 63 =$ _____

$41209 \div 59 =$ _____

$12301 \div 41 =$ _____

$7990 \div 31 =$ _____

$22034 \div 71 =$ _____

$3604 \div 47 =$ _____

$90155 \div 16 =$ _____

$5757 \div 94 =$ _____

$6353 \div 35 =$ _____

$18974 \div 26 =$ _____

$46469 \div 65 =$ _____

$72384 \div 47 =$ _____

$50131 \div 97 =$ _____

$9297 \div 19 =$ _____

$32491 \div 74 =$ _____

$85039 \div 51 =$ _____

Number of Problems: 24   Number Correct: _____   Time to complete: ____ min.

Name: _____

What's Missing?

**2 to 5 Digit Numbers
By 2 Digit Divisors**   **Without Remainders**

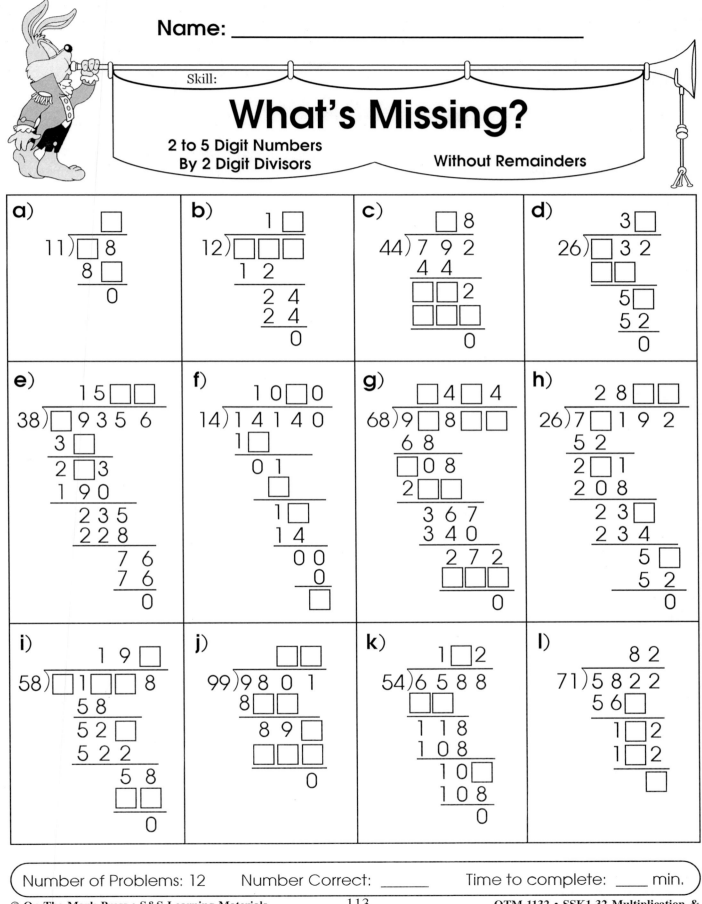

a)
```
        ☐
  11)☐ 8
     8 ☐
       0
```

b)
```
        1 ☐
  12)☐☐☐
     1 2
       2 4
       2 4
         0
```

c)
```
        ☐ 8
  44)7 9 2
     4 4
     ☐☐ 2
     ☐☐☐
         0
```

d)
```
        3 ☐
  26)☐ 3 2
     ☐☐
       5 ☐
       5 2
         0
```

e)
```
        1 5 ☐☐
  38)☐ 9 3 5 6
     3 ☐
     2 ☐ 3
     1 9 0
       2 3 5
       2 2 8
           7 6
           7 6
             0
```

f)
```
        1 0 ☐ 0
  14)1 4 1 4 0
     1 ☐
       0 1
         ☐
         1 ☐
         1 4
           0 0
             0
             ☐
```

g)
```
        ☐ 4 ☐ 4
  68)9 ☐ 8 ☐☐
     6 8
     ☐ 0 8
     2 ☐☐
       3 6 7
       3 4 0
         2 7 2
         ☐☐☐
             0
```

h)
```
        2 8 ☐☐
  26)7 ☐ 1 9 2
     5 2
     2 ☐ 1
     2 0 8
       2 3 ☐
       2 3 4
           5 ☐
           5 2
             0
```

i)
```
        1 9 ☐
  58)☐ 1 ☐☐ 8
     5 8
     5 2 ☐
     5 2 2
         5 8
         ☐☐
           0
```

j)
```
        ☐☐
  99)9 8 0 1
     8 ☐☐
       8 9 ☐
       ☐☐☐
           0
```

k)
```
        1 ☐ 2
  54)6 5 8 8
     ☐☐
     1 1 8
     1 0 8
       1 0 ☐
       1 0 8
           0
```

l)
```
        8 2
  71)5 8 2 2
     5 6 ☐
       1 ☐ 2
       1 ☐ 2
           ☐
```

Number of Problems: 12   Number Correct: _____   Time to complete: ____ min.

Name: _____

What's Missing?

3 to 5 Digit Numbers
By 2 Digit Divisors   With Remainders

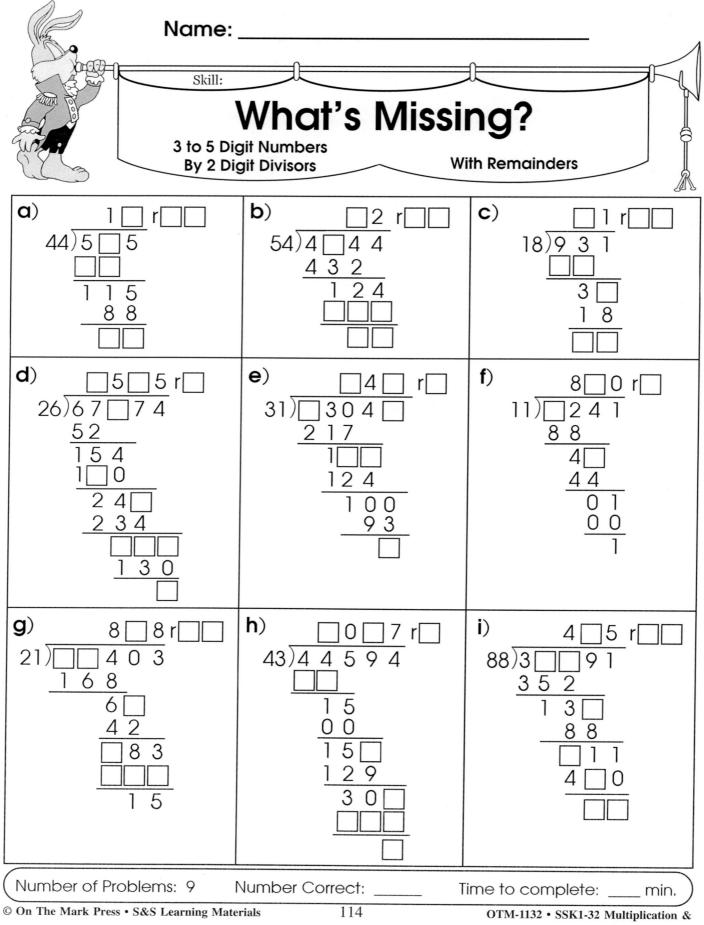

Number of Problems: 9   Number Correct: _____   Time to complete: ____ min.

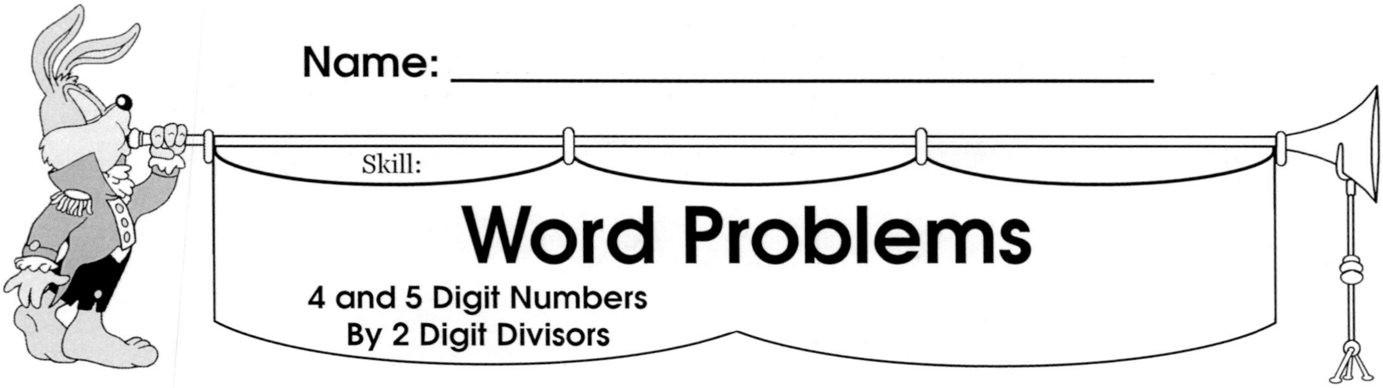

Name: _____

Skill: _____

Word Problems

**4 and 5 Digit Numbers
By 2 Digit Divisors**

27 players came out for the hockey tryouts. A total of 4 401 shots were taken on goal in the first 10 minutes. Coach Hawley was looking for each player to average 180 shots on goal. Did the players accomplish the coach's goal?

The contractor is in the process of digging a hole large enough to install an in-ground pool. The backhoe operator will have to remove approximately 65 000 metric tons of dirt and haul it away in his dump truck. Each dump truck holds 99 metric tons of dirt. How many trips will the dump truck have to take to complete the job?

Kitty Hamleton is a record holder for the fastest land speed achieved by a woman having reached 9 miles per minute in the rocket powered by only three wheels. At this speed, how many hours would it take Kitty to travel 2 700 miles?

96 500 fans were expected to attend this weekend's airplane exhibit. The advertisers are planning to give every 50th person who passes through the gate a free ball cap. How many ball caps should the advertisers plan on giving out?

In late April, 126 anglers registered at the annual smelt fishing derby. The 59 children anglers caught 34 583 smelts and the 67 adults caught 39 195 smelts. Per person, who caught more on average?

Number of Problems: 5   Number Correct: _____   Time to complete: ____ min.

Skill: _____

Number Search

3 to 5 Digit Numbers
By 2 Digit Divisors

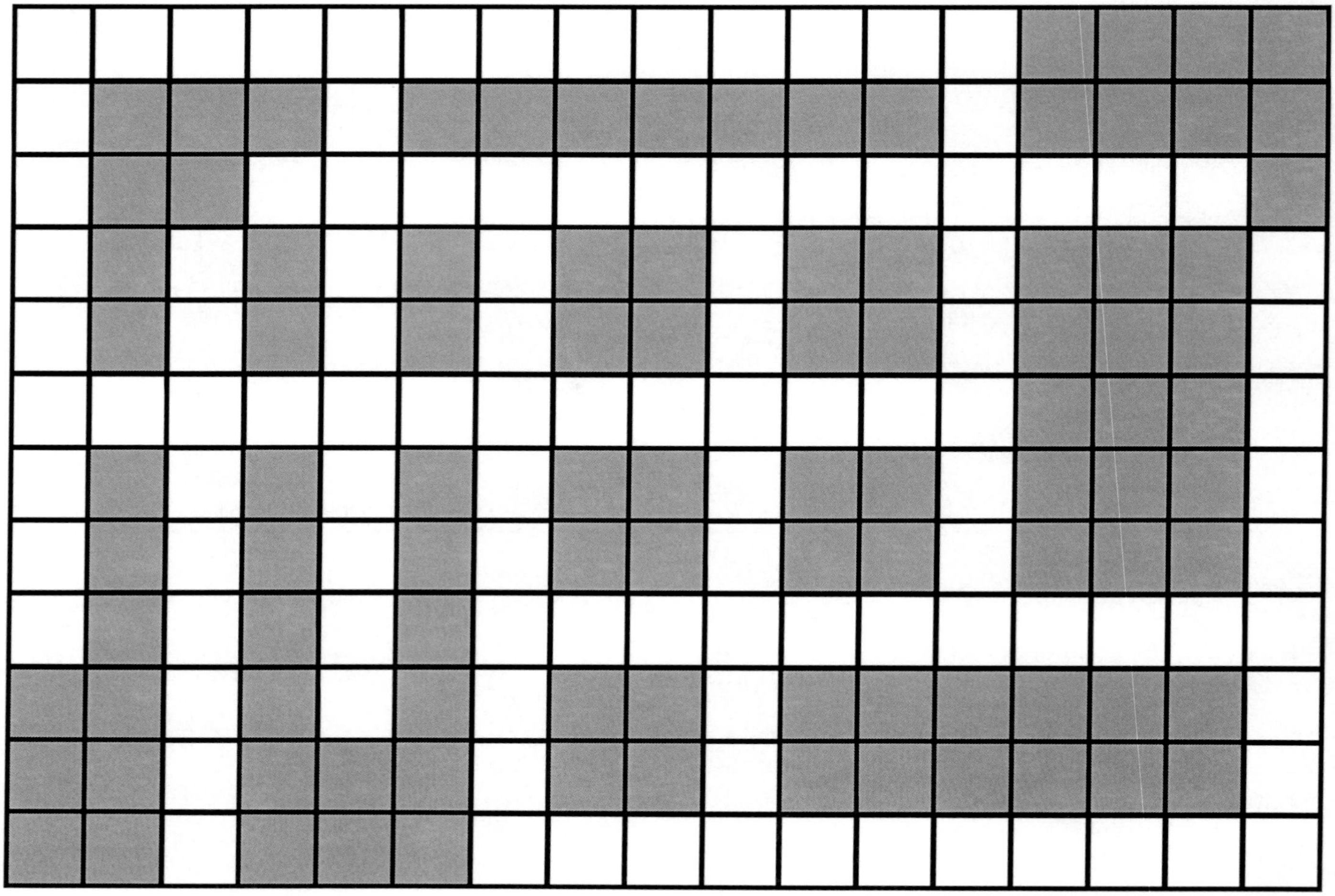

$222 \div 74 =$ ____

$9504 \div 22 =$ ____

$975 \div 65 =$ ____

$836 \div 38 =$ ____

$2376 \div 44 =$ ____

$7029 \div 71 =$ ____

$62050 \div 25 =$ ____

$5841 \div 59 =$ ____

$90987 \div 39 =$ ____

$9074 \div 13 =$ ____

$935 \div 17 =$ ____

$74547 \div 11 =$ ____

Number of Problems: 12   Number Correct: _____   Time to complete: ____ min.

Name: _____

Divisibility Table

**2 to 5 Digit Numbers
By 1 Digit Divisors**

Without Remainders

Circle **yes** if the number is divisable by the given number. Circle **no** if the number is not divisible by the given number.

432			**6 870**			**53 505**			**60**		
by			by			by			by		
4	yes	no	2	yes	no	3	yes	no	2	yes	no
6	yes	no	3	yes	no	4	yes	no	3	yes	no
7	yes	no	6	yes	no	5	yes	no	5	yes	no
8	yes	no	8	yes	no	7	yes	no	6	yes	no
9	yes	no	9	yes	no	9	yes	no	9	yes	no

27 351			**888**			**3 452**			**76 804**		
by			by			by			by		
3	yes	no	2	yes	no	2	yes	no	2	yes	no
4	yes	no	4	yes	no	3	yes	no	3	yes	no
5	yes	no	6	yes	no	4	yes	no	4	yes	no
6	yes	no	8	yes	no	5	yes	no	6	yes	no
7	yes	no	9	yes	no	6	yes	no	8	yes	no

Number of Problems: 40   Number Correct: _____   Time to complete: ____ min.

Name: _____

Decimal Division

1 Digit Whole Number Divisors   Without Remainders

Dividing decimals is very much like dividing whole numbers; the major difference is that before you start dividing, you have to multiply the dividend by a factor of 10 or 100 in order to make it a whole number. Multiply the divisor by the same factor of 10 or 100, and put a decimal point in the quotient (the answer) directly above the new decimal point in the dividend.

$6\overline{)4.20}$	$3\overline{)3.3}$	$9\overline{)8.10}$	$5\overline{)4.50}$	$7\overline{)6.3}$
$4\overline{)4.44}$	$2\overline{)8.0}$	$8\overline{)1.60}$	$3\overline{)3.60}$	$6\overline{)6.0}$
$5\overline{)9.5}$	$7\overline{)1.47}$	$9\overline{)16.2}$	$4\overline{)2.8}$	$8\overline{)6.4}$
$3\overline{)1.20}$	$2\overline{)1.0}$	$6\overline{)3.60}$	$5\overline{)3.50}$	$4\overline{)3.6}$
$8\overline{)6.40}$	$9\overline{)2.7}$	$7\overline{)4.9}$	$2\overline{)12.6}$	$3\overline{)26.4}$
$7\overline{)9.45}$	$5\overline{)7.50}$	$6\overline{)7.80}$	$4\overline{)57.6}$	$9\overline{)91.8}$

Number of Problems: 30   Number Correct: _____   Time to complete: ____ min.

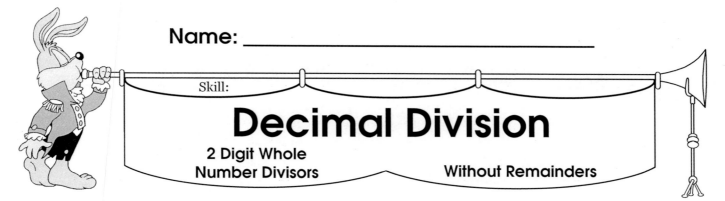

Name: _____

Decimal Division

2 Digit Whole Number Divisors   Without Remainders

Dividing decimals is very much like dividing whole numbers; the major difference is that before you start dividing, you have to multiply the dividend by a factor of 10 or 100 in order to make it a whole number. Multiply the divisor by the same factor of 10 or 100, then put a decimal point in the quotient (the answer) directly above the new decimal point in the dividend.

$22\overline{)13.2}$	$13\overline{)7.8}$	$44\overline{)22.0}$	$38\overline{)19.0}$	$58\overline{)1.16}$
$31\overline{)18.6}$	$71\overline{)35.5}$	$56\overline{)50.4}$	$65\overline{)5.20}$	$34\overline{)3.74}$
$16\overline{)11.2}$	$49\overline{)5.88}$	$26\overline{)4.68}$	$72\overline{)28.8}$	$81\overline{)72.9}$
$79\overline{)6.32}$	$55\overline{)8.80}$	$84\overline{)9.24}$	$19\overline{)36.1}$	$48\overline{)7.68}$
$46\overline{)64.40}$	$12\overline{)1.68}$	$32\overline{)70.4}$	$24\overline{)4.08}$	$73\overline{)8.03}$
$54\overline{)27.0}$	$21\overline{)1.89}$	$88\overline{)5.28}$	$15\overline{)2.25}$	$43\overline{)6.02}$

Number of Problems: 30   Number Correct: _____   Time to complete: ____ min.

Certificate

has done an amazing job on

Multiplication

Keep up the good work!

Teacher

Date

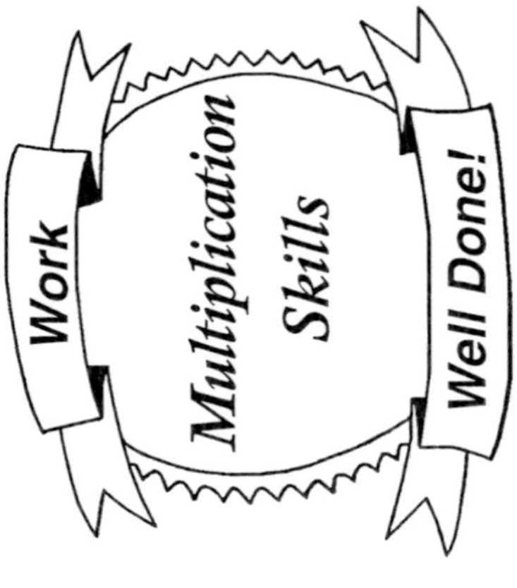

Work

Multiplication Skills

Well Done!

Certificate

has done an amazing job on

Division

Keep up the good work!

Teacher

Date

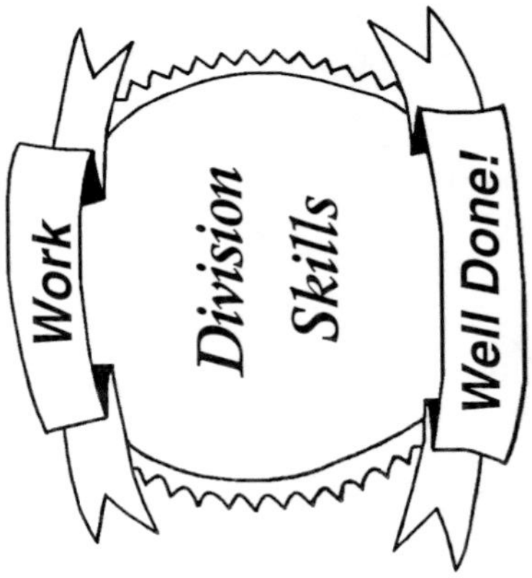

Work

Division Skills

Well Done!

Answer Key
Multiplication Drills

Picture Multiplication: *(page 4)*

32   27   12   6   10   40   12   15

Multiplying With Zero: *(page 5)*

All answers are zero.

Multiplying With One: *(page 6)*

6   2   9   1   12
3   10   7   11   4
5   8   12   3   9
1   6   4   10   8
5   2   11   7   3
12   6   9   4   8

Multiplying With Two: *(page 7)*

14   2   24   18   6
4   20   12   22   8
10   16   24   2   12
6   14   18   8   20
10   4   16   2   24
18   8   6   14   20

Multiplying With Three:
(page 8)

3   33   21   15   6
18   30   9   36   24
12   27   15   24   3
18   30   6   27   12
9   21   33   3   30
36   9   18   27   6

Multiplying With Four:
(page 9)

36   48   4   24   32
8   40   20   44   12
16   28   48   8   20
32   24   44   36   16
12   28   40   4   8
32   12   48   16   36

Multiplying With Five: *(page 10)*

40   5   15   60   10
35   20   55   45   30
50   25   35   10   30
25   55   20   40   5
15   45   60   25   40
35   45   50   5   15

Multiplying With Six: *(page 11)*

36   6   48   30   72
54   60   18   42   12
66   24   48   72   6
42   60   30   72   54
66   6   36   24   48
54   72   42   12   30

Multiplying With Seven:
(page 12)

35   84   7   21   70
63   14   42   56   28
49   77   14   35   56
42   7   21   84   28
63   77   49   70   63
49   35   84   7   21

Multiplying With Eight:
(page 13)

40   72   96   24   56
8   48   16   88   64
80   32   8   24   40
64   88   48   16   72
56   32   80   96   56
40   8   64   96   72

Multiplying With Nine:
(page 14)

81   108 45   9   54
63   90   18   36   72
27   99   63   45   108
36   72   99   18   54
9   90   27   81   72
45   108 81   63   27

Multiplying With Ten:
(page 15)

80   50   30   90   10
20   100 70   40   120
110 60   30   70   40
90   100 20   60   50
80   10   110 70   100
20   50   70   120 40

Multiplying With Eleven:
(page 16)

66   121 11   77   55
33   110 44   88   22
132 99   55   11   121
33   77   44   110 88
22   66   99   132 121
77   99   55   11   33

Multiplying With Twelve:
(page 17)

144 84   48   12   108
60   24   132 36   96
120 72   84   60   120
108 144 36   12   72
96   132 48   120 24
60   84   144 36   108

Multiplication Review:
(page 18)

15   16   4   42   72   4
56   0   14   40   35   2
24   108 18   44   8   60
84   21   14   54   63   90
9   10   36   49   45   66
40   27   81   77   18   16

Multiplication Wheels:
(page 20)

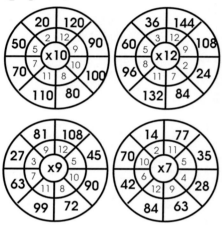

Single Digit Multiplication:
(page 21)

10   77   16   72   54
14   56   36   63   35
36   66   40   20   56
18   63   36   32   8
45   15   48   12   3
25   8   27   21   18

Single Digit Multiplication :
(page 22)

28   48   48   86   55
88   88   68   69   99
12   39   80   55   93
96   84   28   24   66
46   90   26   60   62
80   66   80   68   82

Single Digit Multiplication :
(page 23)

801 161 63   420 6
30   630 45   196 7
150 270 72   608 16
144 108 18   295 24
144 36   48   468 265
4   168 2   21   234

Rocket Ship Multiplication: *(page 24)*

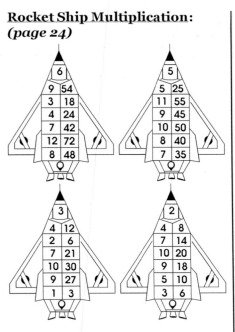

Single Digit Multiplication: *(page 25)*

148	280	66	64	385
69	126	264	112	366
328	102	144	276	42
168	581	50	504	217
365	448	78	216	531
42	81	365	198	477

Single Digit Multiplication: *(page 26)*

365	198	60	477	52	240
32	84	150	252	84	368
171	144	148	69	328	168
385	42	280	64	308	126
264	112	366	190	102	144
350	581	50			

Multiplication Wheels: *(page 27)*

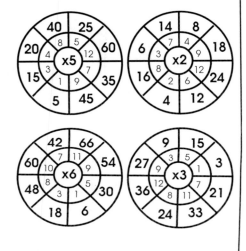

Float the Boats: *(page 28)*

72	9	6	7	369	224
12	369	175	5	8	104
200	5	3	147	266	133

Word Problems: *(page 29)*

$7 \times 2 = 14$ $6 \times 84 = 504$

$225 \times 3 = 675$ $17 \times 12 = 204$

Single Digit Multiplication: *(page 30)*

468	204	336	264
64	855	320	168
288	162	210	275
738	259	792	702
432	696	78	288
360	288	558	174
675	340	760	462

More Rocket Ship Multiplication: *(page 31)*

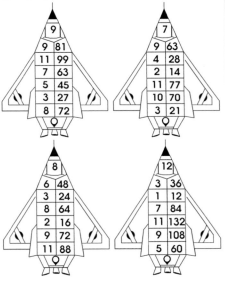

Single Digit Multiplication: *(page 32)*

244	158	405	108
328	222	144	261
182	128	88	225
696	72	135	24
75	220	276	486
36	188	70	680
71	152	56	392

Multiplication Review: *(page 33)*

12	63	2	51	102	84
19	121	28	250	198	52
136	175	176	36	15	49
48	60	81	36	45	100
120	68	108	84	21	78
0	72	12			

Two Digit Multiplication: *(page 34)*

1 406	966	3 157	540	735
1 584	684	340	4 312	3 770
132	864	8 460	700	979
1 653	352	240	540	4 950
4 512	1 156	7 840	315	4 617
4 582	1 692	2 496	396	7 743

Word Problems: *(page 35)*

$27 \times 45 = 1\ 215$

$56 \times 12 = 672$

$16 \times 12 = 192$

$\$23.00 \times 52 = \$1\ 196.00$

Multiplication Review: *(page 36)*

310	153	324	752	245	540
99	474	108	231	142	36
158	182	252	160	48	595
168	680	704	324	128	72
184	696	285	80	330	130
220	504	106	368	344	450

You're A Star: *(page 37)*

33	120	162
364	102	289
174	135	558
121	680	494
1 326	1 728	2 109

Pyramid Factors: *(page 38)*

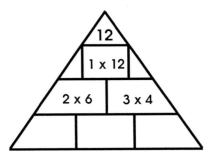

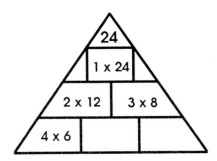

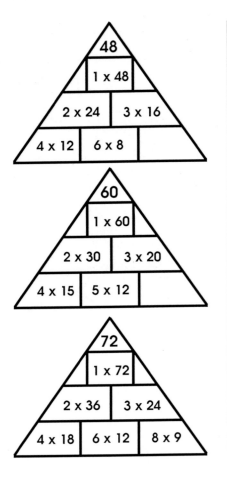

Banner Multiplication:
(page 48)

152	162	222	222
5 695	1 863	1 568	3 634
10 479	32 298	11 286	20 736
131 376	254 698	57 960	335 552

Three Digit Multiplication:
(page 49)

97 929	559 215	26 883
614 383	208 638	404 424
113 398	459 250	60 417
225 630	253 380	684 250
127 544	439 470	61 375
152 532	217 566	206 647
529 930	164 190	

Balloon Multiplication:
(page 42)

820	513	756	2 805	6 318
594	56	400		

Word Problems: *(page 43)*

4 x $14.98 = $59.92
63 x 17 = 1 071
$0.25 x 216 = $54.00
5 x 31 = 155

Bubble Multiplication:
(page 44)

2 100	1 036	589	
2 080	8 448	175	
153	891	630	273

Multiplication Review:
(page 45)

828	1 092	918
1 785	1 480	2 632
1 408	869	120
630	2 907	2 656
3 540	992	429
990	3 952	665
6 004	3 380	4 680
378	888	2 024
784	370	513
792	1 113	1 566
3 772	3 960	1 950

Lunch Bag Multiplication:
(page 46)
Answers may vary.

Two Digit Multiplication:
(page 47)

186 714	469 474	677 312
136 462	111 375	216 120
29 470	2 604	38 571
513 126	667 992	475 083
31 396	281 648	646 848
94 068	584 610	3 076
53 568	660 744	

Multiplication Review - Two & Three Digit Numbers: *(page 50)*

5 880	5 643
423 582	773 508
3 159	5 877 228
984 378	7 038 104
4 319 104	5 799 066
49 383	23 754
6 392	9 875
22 176	113 523
18 711	700 016
2 762 904	2 664 498

Three Digit Multiplication:
(page 51)

1 692 558	3 76920	651 168
135 344	529 248	12 792
105 078	806 403	788 168
2 400 891	4 944 064	153 690
3 395 295	215 468	666 036
1 922 120	4 440 954	555 120
143 500	457 056	

Three Digit Multiplication:
(page 52)

3 828 870	6 550 809	3 940 800
1 986 175	5 685 332	5 689 710
42 084	3 408 135	47 674
1 230 780	1 998 495	22 375
1 038 726	177 606	68 162
5 345 400	719 740	2 426 775
362 340	259 506	

Two Digit Multiplication:
(page 39)

798	552	969	2 001	209
1 900	476	768	4 536	2 072
2 211	5 175	4 704	8 536	3 599
1 615	3 003	4 042	5 022	551
414	1 296	2 652	7 055	3 808

Picture Puzzles: *(page 40)*

6 x $2.75 = $16.50
6 x $13.79 = $82.74
27 x $1.50 = $40.50
9 x $12.79 = $115.11

Even More Rocket Ship Multiplication: *(page 41)*

OTM-1132 • SSK1-32 Multiplication & Division Drills

Word Problems: *(page 53)*

276 x 38 = 10 488
$5.75 x 347 = $1 995.25
212 x $27.25 = $5 777.00
64 756 x 30 = 1 942 680

What's Missing?: *(page 54)*

```
   309          94          925
  x 242        x 37        x 233
  -----        ----        -----
   618         658         2775
  1236         282         2775
   618        ----         1850
 ------       3 478        ------
 74 778                   215 525
```

```
    97           84          17
  x 20         x 37        x 45
  ----         ----        ----
     0          588          85
  1940          252          68
 ------         ----        ----
  1 940        3 108         765
```

```
   377          51           44
  x 26         x 55         x 16
  ----         ----         ----
  2262          255          264
   754          255           44
  ----         ----         ----
  9 802        2 805         704
```

```
  5422         6710         9441
   x 43         x 25         x 17
 ------        -----        -----
  16266        33550        66087
 21688        13420         9441
 -------      ------        ------
 233 146      167 750      160 497
```

Multiplication Review: *(page 55)*

15 500 856	7 701 840	36 721 152
76 019 973	2 948 400	3 784 158
60 238 126	1 196 601	18 818 744
1 217 711	1 075 410	891 077
1 539 078	13 096 944	1 902 310

Find the Multiples: *(page 56)*

9

11	18	36	20		12
16	32		45		9
81	54	43	63	90
4	99	27	108	

7

9	14	64	42		58
13	84		21		77
39	18		35	90
41	26	49	63	

3

11	6	17	33		30
27	42		21		51
36	19	62	16	25
24	40	45		

11

24	30	57	64		12
22	54		55		77
33	43		121	11
88	99	27	66	

8

27	72	57	16		22
24	5		48		88
32	97	8	81	80
43	40	64	101	17

5

25	21	5	19		10
32	65		45		26
15	64	40	50	48
55	91	70	100	

Multiplying Decimals: *(page 57)*

0.44	0.0011	0.0621	1.0031
0.033	0.0294	0.0016	0.1591
3.7051	2.0212	31.496	35.9941
49.3564	9.12	25.026	3.6856
10.842	6.4764	3.633	1.54
1.392	53.04	0.0054	0.1152

Multiplying Money: *(page 58)*

$1 452.17	$14 323.18	$234.96
$7 830.26	$58.75	$25 258.99
$5 111.68	$3 117.66	$5 607.50
$3 267.99	$10 051.66	$48 265.44
$8 198.34	$1 519.04	$5 117.32

Multiplying Decimals: *(page 59)*

402.1556	2 717.3124	405.8115
2 092.1428	57.78	2 165.0769
3 260.3345	130.1248	87.8094
1 320.41	181.1964	8.2779
7 579.2	1.0395	59.7014

Division Drills

Picture Division: (page 62)

2 groups, 2	4 groups, 4
6 groups, 6	2 groups, 2

Division ÷1: (page 63)

5	9	1	6	2		
0	7	8	4	3		
7	9	5	8	6		
6	3	9		0	8	2
5	4	7		1	9	0
6	5	2				

Division ÷2: (page 64)

3	1	5	6	8	
6	18	1	10	24	
12	6	2	12		
2	5			12	2
9	10			6	18
14	8				
18	9	2	9		

Division ÷3: (page 65)

6	3	10	15	9	
1	5	18	2	24	
15	5	3	15		
4	3			6	8
10	18			15	5
12	9				
30	10	3	10		

Division ÷4: (page 66)

3	6	1	12	7	
8	4	40	9	2	
28	7	4	7		
4	4			8	12
40	8			3	7
36	2				
44	11	4	44		

Division ÷5: (page 67)

2	30	10	5	8	
15	6	20	1	35	
45	9	5	45		
7	15			1	4
11	5			2	8
30	9				
60	12	5	12		

Division ÷6: (page 68)

5	6	7	10	18	
24	2	48	6	9	
36	6	6	6		
6	8			12	4
54	42			5	1
10	3				
60	10	6	60		

Division ÷7: (page 69)

4	70	2	7	3
7	6	35	9	8
63	9	7	63	
3	5		7	6

56	63		7	28
10	2			
49	7	7	7	

Division ÷8: (page 70)

24	1	7	4	64
2	40	80	9	6
32	4	8	32	
8	8		2	48
9	3		32	56
80	5			
64	8	8	8	

Division ÷9: (page 71)

27	1	5	9	54
2	72	7	4	90
45	5	9	45	
2	10		36	63
8	9		6	9
3	45			
63	7	9	7	

Division Review One: (page 72)

3	18	36	8	9
3	32	12	9	7
10	8	6	45	9
7	32	30	4	2
48	22	10	27	14
9	63	6	40	3

Division Review Two: (page 73)

4	9	10	15	64	7
6	54	7	18	40	6
36	36	21	3	6	9
16	12	9	56	18	5
18	9	15	10	12	9

What's Missing?: (page 74)

a) *10's:* 6, 6
b) *10's:* 3, 3   *1's:* 2
c) *10's:* 2   *1's:* 8, 8
d) *10's:* 4   *1's:* 8
e) *10's:* 3, 0   *1's:* 9
f) *10's:* 6   *1's:* 5
g) *10's:* 4   *1's:* 0
h) *10's:* 6   *1's:* 3, 8, 0
i) *10's:* 1, 1   *1's:* 0, 0
j) *10's:* 1   *1's:* 5, 5, 0
k) *100's:* 1   *10's:* 1, 2
   1's: 2, 4
l) *10's:* 1, 0   *1's:* 0, 0, 0

Word Problems: (page 75)

7	22	6	6
7	8	12	10
12	4		

One Digit Division: (page 76)

12	11	24	20	109
58	91	2	13	129
17	15	52	77	81
30	45	25	68	125
142	124	116	180	72

One Digit Division: (page 77)

18	22	12
483	0	110
16	154	86
16	9	49
72	19	411
114	0	5
80	23	65
22	44	7
111	170	90
11	38	33

One Digit Division: (page 78)

9 r1	13 r2	1 r4	33 r1	11 r5
110 r1	107 r1	31 r2	10 r5	129 r4
22 r1	182 r1	81 r5	12 r4	97 r1
332 r2	2 r8	85 r3	37 r5	9 r1
6 r2	83 r7	4 r4	46 r1	110 r1

One Digit Division: (page 79)

25 r2	72 r4	75 r7
10 r4	71 r6	132 r1
97 r2	12 r5	53 r1
212 r1	2 r3	40 r1
314 r2	132 r4	11 r5
151 r1	3 r5	144 r5
38 r1	76 r4	14 r1
455 r1	11 r3	65 r4
235 r2	92 r4	5 r1
15 r6	84 r3	13 r2

One Digit Division: (page 80)

111	56	411	185	30
1 006	133	157	37	1 273
401	926	49	589	74
289	279	106	1 896	1 226

One Digit Division: (page 81)

4 248	1 374	81
50	2 160	183
500	133	926
158	482	444
193	128	1 104
151	401	1 266
1 173	21	706
661	98	1 439
202	1 671	491
1 680	483	819

One Digit Division: (page 82)

73 r2	71 r4	990 r5
43 r1	332 r1	
1 550 r1	140 r1	1 852 r3
21 r4	400 r4	
90 r2	556 r6	1 896 r2
244 r3	81 r5	
791 r7	960 r3	499 r1
793 r4	1 645 r3	

One Digit Division: (page 83)

134 r1	2 970 r1	47 r4
1 883 r2	130 r4	483 r7
50 r3	640 r4	33 r2
793 r4	405 r1	263 r2

373 r7   1 191 r4   38 r2
1 019 r2   639 r1   241 r1
706 r1   4 827 r1   57 r1
238 r4   904 r8   998 r5
376 r5   566 r1   1 055 r1
157 r3   2 330 r2   1 295 r2

One Digit Division: (page 84)
1 218   909   623
928   1 111
258   6 484   916
19 913   974
9 740   356   20 823
1 446   2 124
10 331   38 230   362
13 925   7 407

One Digit Division: (page 85)
701   30 714   742
10 154   1 055   154
12 981   7 806   843
13 511   32 077   20 824
454   4 114   844
17 884   6 901   1 269
17 719   19 797   19 147
1 931   5 386   2 499
3 937   10 158   13 908
2 293   29 711   6 339

One Digit Division: (page 86)
359 r3   37 710 r1   8 473 r1
772 r3   31 441 r2
6 235 r8   1 435 r2   5 220 r2
3 293 r4   2 080 r1
16 589 r2   863 r3   583 r1
15 285 r1   10 389 r4
1 428 r3   43 829 r1   685 r5
7 732 r1   11 790 r7

One Digit Division: (page 87)
307 r5   12 809 r3   750 r8
12 299 r2   1 394 r5   37 385 r1
444 r1   19 549 r3   642 r6
13 863 r3   1 025 r4   4 272 r2
1 241 r4   43 723 r1   15 447 r3
4 642 r3   539 r4   13 775 r2
779 r3   2 972 r3   9 990 r2
14 268 r4   378 r3   46 728 r1
1 577 r2   29 429 r1   7 214 r8
1 222 r3   3 820 r5   5 082 r3

Division Review Three: (page 88)
11   135   1 023
22 810   71
449   3 372   2 133
281   10 928
89   5 477   641
23   661
93   1 087   9 054
223   311

Division Review Four: (page 89)
237   11 111   404
19   434   6 034

130   6 914   1 165
7   1 356   3 374
76   26 374   294
9 919   219   579
16   10 326   9
545   14 154   91
2 374   619   2 830
5   772   10 438

Division Review Five: (page 90)
7 267 r3   54 r1   576 r2
34 r3   22 r3
1 049 r3   3 562 r7   8 r5
1 465 r2   9 059 r6
117 r5   2 260 r1   13 049 r1
555 r1   1 344 r1
3 669 r7   121 r6   456 r3
8 r1   12 757 r4

Division Review Six: (page 91)
82 r1   3 230 r2   30 r3
399 r1   7 220 r4   1 r5
4 068 r8   203 r3   616 r3
717 r2   3 660 r1   9 r2
1 916 r2   17 260 r1   80 r2
5 592 r1   1 621 r2   87 r5
1 080 r1   13 316 r6   44 r3
13 580 r4   2 040 r3   8 257 r5
8 r3   1 866 r1   10 104 r1
66 r6   19 996 r4   7 874 r3

What's Missing?: (page 92)
a) 1 000's: 2   10's: 5, 2
   1's: 7
b) 100's: 4   10's: 8
   1's: 5, 5
c) 1 000's: 4   100's: 1
   10's: 6   1's: 9, 2
d) 10's: 2, 8, 4, 4, 4   1's: 2
e) 10 000's: 6   1 000's: 5, 6
   100's: 4, 2   10's: 1
   1's: 4, 2
f) 10 000's: 1   100's: 1
   10's: 8, 8
g) 10 000's: 3, 1   1 000's: 2
   10's: 1   1's: 7, 4, 4
h) 1 000's: 8, 2, 2   100's: 3, 3
   10's: 2   1's: 4, 0

What's Missing?: (page 93)
a) 10's: 7, 1, 2   1's: 1, 3
b) 1 000's: 6   100's: 9, 5
   10's: 7   1's: 8 r 4
c) 10's: 9   1's: 8, 2 r 2
d) 100's: 5, 6   10's: 3, 8 r 3
e) 1 000's: 4, 4   100's: 5, 4
   1's: 6, 7 r 7
f) 10 000's: 4   1 000's: 8
   100's: 7, 3, 7   10's: 2
   1's: 1
g) 10 000's: 7   1 000's: 1, 2, 4
   100's: 9, 4   10's: 9 r 1

h) 1 000's: 6, 5   100's: 7, 6, 6
   10's: 4   1's: 8, 5 r 5

Word Problems: (page 94)
2 535   312   yes   1 940   412

Divisibility Table: (page 95)
64:    yes   no   no   no   yes
112:    yes   no   no   yes   no
600:    yes   yes   yes   yes   no
90:    yes   no   yes   yes   yes
228:    yes   yes   no   no   no
552:    yes   yes   yes   yes   no
696:    yes   yes   yes   no   yes
808:    yes   no   yes   no   no

Divisibility Table: (page 96)
1 747:   no   no   no   no   no
98 400:   yes   yes   yes   yes   yes
15 051:   yes   no   no   no   no
2 355:   no   yes   no   no   no
11 606:   yes   no   no   yes   no
5 428:   yes   no   no   no   no
8 989:   no   no   no   no   no
67 401:   yes   no   no   no   no

Two Digit Division: (page 97)
4   5   9   3
4   2   7   3
4   2   7   5
2   3   4   2
3   3   5   2

Two Digit Division: (page 98)
2   2   5   3   2   4
3   1   4   2   3   2
3   7   3   2   2   1
2   6   6   2   4   3

Two Digit Division: (page 99)
4 r3   3 r6   3 r4   4 r1
3 r3   7 r4   1 r1   1 r4
2 r9   1 r5   1 r15   4 r2
4 r15   5 r4   2 r24   1 r9
1 r1   1 r21   2 r15   3 r11

Two Digit Division: (page 100)
5 r14   1 r24   1 r13
3 r4   2 r1   2 r6
1 r6   2 r11   1 r10
1 r1   1 r19   3 r7
2 r10   4 r18   2 r18
1 r10   1 r8   5 r11
2 r3   2 r22   3 r5
1 r13   7 r1   1 r36

Two Digit Division: (page 101)
18   2   8   3
6   1   42   7
2   68   2   15
10   6   5   17
4   38   1   5

Two Digit Division: (page 102)

6	4	16	3	5	24
2	9	20	12	1	23
11	3	5	4	3	21
19	2	22	7	4	22

Two Digit Division: (page 103)

28 r 15	1 r 6	39 r 5	7 r 33
19 r 5	1 r 9	9 r 91	5 r 9
31 r 20	8 r 53	2 r 1	22 r 7
2 r 12	5 r 6	28 r 7	1 r 50
17 r 47	20 r 8	5 r 34	24 r 2

Two Digit Division: (page 104)

15 r 18	4 r 18	21 r 5
20 r 11	1 r 27	36 r 14
17 r 12	4 r 45	24 r 12
2 r 26	1 r 3	9 r 8
37 r 8	2 r 24	6 r 10
8 r 22	4 r 36	4 r 57
20 r 33	2 r 10	1 r 46
2 r 7	35 r 24	45 r 6

Two Digit Division: (page 105)

8	100	303	13
54	56	86	6
3	198	17	198
90	19	93	52
48	187	156	'124

Two Digit Divison: (page 106)

22	24	60	9	125	5
71	19	78	92	23	127
268	6	13	24	74	90
32	58	13	55	136	54

Two Digit Division: (page 107)

10 r 7	20 r 3	97 r 57	189 r 8
92 r 55	56 r 15	12 r 12	65 r 13
779 r 7	25 r 27	4 r 76	9 r 5
18 r 45	86 r 22	79 r 5	6 r 24
33 r 4	457 r 8	10 r 4	198 r 23

Two Digit Division: (page 108)

119 r 47	9 r 10	36 r 90
16 r 9	60 r 20	14 r 30
14 r 29	45 r 12	16 r 20
99 r 5	10 r 7	105 r 11
178 r 27	12 r 5	12 r 3
18 r 35	3 r 36	73 r 7
22 r 36	156 r 20	85 r 36
39 r 24	119 r 50	102 r 56

Two Digit Division: (page 109)

156	1 001	48	5 500
276	67	434	23
165	1 928	283	3 842
2 083	54	173	1 656
104	298	1 076	342

Two Digit Division: (page 110)

60	155	169
977	5 200	120
1 081	115	86
2 222	202	1 421

1 636	676	221
345	340	440
5 066	247	812
632	240	585

Two Digit Division: (page 111)

124 r 26	1 032 r 1	73 r 18
1 190 r 50		
1 498 r 3	90 r 50	485 r 17
122 r 6		
72 r 13	851 r 7	148 r 32
701 r 10		
987 r 13	142 r 16	1 169 r 61
136 r 15		
25 r 25	1 453 r 6	44 r 25
966 r 4		

Two Digit Division: (page 112)

103 r 5	291 r 35	409 r 6
406 r 71	6 958 r 5	73 r 12
566 r 87	146 r 22	128 r 39
698 r 27	300 r 1	257 r 23
310 r 24	76 r 32	5 634 r 11
61 r 23	181 r 18	729 r 20
714 r 59	1 540 r 4	516 r 79
489 r 6	439 r 5	1 667 r 22

What's Missing?: (page 113)

a) 10's: 8   1's: 8, 8
b) 100's: 1   10's: 4
   1's: 2, 4
c) 100's: 3, 3   10's: 1, 5, 5
   1's: 2
d) 100's: 8, 7   10's: 8
   1's: 2, 2
e) 10 000's: 5   1 000's: 8, 1
   10's: 6   1's: 2
f) 1 000's: 4   100's: 0
   10's: 1, 4   1's: 0
g) 10 000's: 2   1 000's: 1, 8, 7
   100's: 2, 2   10's: 5, 7, 7
   1's: 2, 2
h) 1 000's: 5, 3   10's: 9, 9
   1's: 2, 2
i) 10 000's: 1   100's: 0
   10's: 7, 7, 5   1's: 1, 8
j) 100's: 9, 8   10's: 9, 1, 9
   1's: 9, 1, 1
k) 1 000's: 5   100's: 4
   10's: 2   1's: 8
l) 10's: 8, 4, 4   1's: 0

What's Missing?: (page 114)

a) 100's: 4   10's: 5, 4, 2
   1's: 2, 7 r 27
b) 100's: 4, 1   10's: 8, 0, 1
   1's: 8, 6 r 16
c) 100's: 9   10's: 5, 0, 1
   1's: 1, 3 r 13
d) 1 000's: 2, 3   100's: 4, 1
   10's: 9, 7, 3   1's: 4, 4 r 4
e) 10 000's: 2   100's: 7, 3
   10's: 4   1's: 3, 0, 7 r 7

f) 1 000's: 9   10's: 4, 4 r 1
g) 10 000's: 1   1 000's: 7
   100's: 1, 1   10's: 2, 0, 6
   1's: 8 r 15
h) 10 000's: 4   1 000's: 1, 3
   100's: 3   10's: 3, 9, 0
   1's: 4, 1, 3 r 3
i) 1 000's: 6   100's: 5, 5
   10's: 1, 9, 4, 7   1's: 1 r 71

Word Problems: (page 115)

163, no	657	5	1 930

The children (586.15)

Number Search: (page 116)

```
9 0 9 8 7 ÷ 3 9 = 2 3 3 3
3       0                 2
5     6 2 0 5 0 ÷ 2 5 = 2 4 8 2
÷ 9 9 8     3     2               8
1 7     ÷ 4     7         ÷       3
7 4 5 4 7 ÷ 1 1 = 6 7 7 7         6
= ÷ 1     ÷     ÷     4         ÷
5 6 =     5     4         =       3
5 5 9     9 0 7 4 ÷ 1 3 = 6 9 8
= 9 =     =                   =
1       9       5               2
5         9 5 0 4 ÷ 2 2 = 4 3 2
```

Divisibility Table: (page 117)

432:	yes	yes	no	yes	yes
6 870:	yes	yes	yes	no	no
53 505:	yes	no	yes	no	yes
60:	yes	yes	yes	yes	no
27 351:	yes	no	no	no	no
888:	yes	yes	yes	yes	no
3 542:	yes	no	yes	no	no
76 804:	yes	no	yes	no	no

Decimal Division: (page 118)

0.7	1.1	0.9	0.9	0.9
1.11	4.0	0.2	1.2	1.0
1.9	0.21	1.8	0.7	0.8
0.4	0.5	0.6	0.7	0.9
0.8	0.3	0.7	6.3	8.8
1.35	1.5	1.3	14.4	10.2

Decimal Divison: (page 119)

0.6	0.6	0.5	0.5	0.02
0.6	0.5	0.9	0.08	0.11
0.7	0.12	0.18	0.4	0.9
0.08	0.16	0.11	1.9	0.16
1.4	0.14	2.2	0.17	0.11
0.5	0.09	0.06	0.15	0.14